MW00998089

QUICK COURSE®

in

MICROSOFT®

PowerPoint®

2000

Fast-track training® for busy people

JOYCE COX

POLLY URBAN

PUBLISHED BY
Online Press
15442 Bel-Red Road
Redmond, WA 98052
Phone: (425) 885-1441, (800) 854-3344
Fax: (425) 881-1642
E-mail: quickcourse@otsiweb.com
Web site: www.quickcourse.com

Publisher's Cataloging-in-Publication
(Provided by Quality Books, Inc.)

Cox, Joyce.
    Quick Course in Microsoft PowerPoint 2000 /
    Joyce Cox, Polly Urban. -- 1st ed.
    p. cm. -- (Quick Course books)
    Includes index.
    ISBN: 1-58278-004-8

    1. Microsoft PowerPoint (Computer file)   2.
Computer graphics.   3. Business presentations--
Graphic methods--Computer programs.   I. Urban,
Polly.   II. Title.   III. Title: Microsoft
PowerPoint 2000   IV. Series.

    T385.C69 1999   006.6'869
                    QBI99-500177
                         99-070318
                           CIP

Printed and bound in the United States of America.

1 2 3 4 5 6 7 8 9 I P I P 3 2 1 0

Content overview

PART ONE: LEARNING THE BASICS

PART TWO: BUILDING PROFICIENCY

Content details

PART ONE: LEARNING THE BASICS

PART TWO: BUILDING PROFICIENCY

LEARNING THE BASICS

In Part One, we cover basic techniques for working with Microsoft PowerPoint. After completing these three chapters, you'll know enough to be able to create and deliver simple presentations. In Chapter 1, you create a simple presentation using the AutoContent Wizard, and you learn how to edit slides and incorporate special effects. In Chapter 2, you add clip art, apply animation, and create a graph to make your presentation more eye-catching. In Chapter 3, you base a new presentation on a design template, edit and format the slides, and learn the basics for delivering a presentation, including via the Internet or an intranet.

1

Creating a Simple Presentation

You use the AutoContent Wizard as a starting point for a simple presentation. Then you edit the presentation's slides and learn how to apply special effects. Finally, we show you how to get help and how to quit PowerPoint.

The presentation you create in this chapter is about a new line of tour packages for a travel agency. You can easily adapt the presentation to any new product or service.

Presentation created and concepts covered:

Use the AutoContent Wizard to create a presentation that you can customize

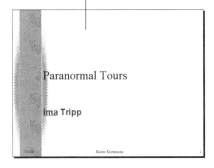

Paranormal Tours

Ima Tripp

Exotic Excursions

Objectives
- **To provide new tour packages for affiliated agencies**
- **To satisfy the public's increasing interest in the paranormal**

Exotic Excursions

Replace the text provided with your own title and bulleted items

Customer Requirements
- **Tours that are not only insightful but enjoyable**
- **Tours that focus on the latest developments in paranormalism**
- **Tour packages that are flexible**

Exotic Excursions

Some Sample Tours
- **Ghostly Bed and Breakfasts**
  - **Europe**
  - **United States**
- **Mythical Monsters**
- **Extraterrestrial Exploration**

Exotic Excursions

Promote and demote bulleted items to create subordinate lists

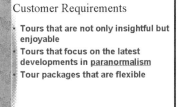

Customer Sirvey
- **Over the last dekade, public interest in paranormal phenomena has increased 40%**

Exotic Excursions

Rap Up
- **By endorsing the Paranormal Tours line, Exotic Excrusions Incorporated will be at the forfront of worldwide travel agencies**

Exotic Excursions

Use special effects to animate your slides and build bulleted lists

Quickly produce a sophisticated presentation with start-to-finish design consistency

I f you conducted a survey of people who use computers as part of their jobs, you would probably find that most of the survey respondents work with one or two programs most of the time, with another couple of programs every so often, and with a few programs once in a blue moon. And of the respondents who have some kind of presentation program installed on their computers, most would put that program in the second or, more likely, the third category. Very few people develop presentations for a living, and for most people, developing presentations is not a big enough part of their jobs to warrant spending hours becoming an expert.

Fortunately, a sophisticated presentation package like Microsoft PowerPoint 2000 provides a lot of support for its users. If you are faced with the task of creating a presentation, you can focus on its message and leave the aesthetic details to PowerPoint. In fact, PowerPoint can even help you structure the content of the presentation so that you can successfully get your message across.

Throughout this book, we focus on how to use PowerPoint to produce simple yet effective presentations. Because adequate planning and smooth delivery are essential if you want your presentations to have maximum impact, we weave these topics into the chapters where appropriate. By the time you have worked your way through this book, you'll know not only how to use PowerPoint, but how to develop and deliver a presentation that accomplishes your goals.

We assume that you have already installed PowerPoint on your computer. We also assume that you've worked with Microsoft Windows before and that you know how to start programs, move windows, choose commands from menus, highlight text, and so on. If you are a new Windows user, we suggest you take a look at *Quick Course® in Microsoft Windows*, which will help you come up to speed.

It's time to get started, so let's fire up PowerPoint:

1. Choose Programs and then Microsoft PowerPoint from the Windows Start menu.

Other ways to start PowerPoint

Instead of starting PowerPoint by choosing it from the Start menu, you can create a shortcut icon for PowerPoint on your desktop. Right-click a blank area of the desktop and choose New and then Shortcut from the shortcut menu. Then in the Create Shortcut dialog box, click the Browse button, navigate to C:\Program Files\Microsoft Office\Office\ powerpnt, and click Next. Type a name for the shortcut icon and click Finish. For maximum efficiency, you can start PowerPoint and open an existing presentation by choosing the presentation from the Documents submenu of the Start menu, where Windows stores the names of up to 15 of the most recently opened files. If you are using Microsoft Office 2000, you can also choose Open Office Document from the top of the Start menu and navigate to the folder in which the presentation you want to open is stored. To start PowerPoint and open a new presentation, you can choose New Office Document from the top of the Start menu and then double-click the Blank Presentation icon.

2. If necessary, click the Office Assistant's Start Using Microsoft PowerPoint option. (We discuss the Office Assistant on page 24. As you work through this chapter, the Office Assistant may entertain you with some cute antics and may display a message or a light bulb. Other than responding to messages by clicking an option, you can ignore it for now.) PowerPoint then displays this dialog box:

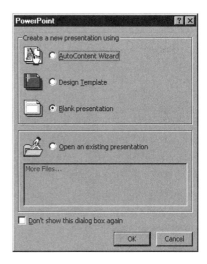

As you can see, you can start a new presentation in one of three ways, or you can open an existing presentation.

Using the AutoContent Wizard

Suppose you are the director of a travel agency called Exotic Excursions. You are pitching a new tour line to management, and you want to create a presentation that will explain the various tours and get people excited about the line. You are using PowerPoint for the first time, and you want to take advantage of all the help you can get. For your first presentation, you're going to let the AutoContent Wizard be your guide. The AutoContent Wizard asks a few questions to get the ball rolling and then allows you to select one of its ready-made presentations as a starting point. You can then customize the presentation's slides by adding, deleting, or changing various elements. Follow the steps on the next page to use the Auto-Content Wizard. (To use the AutoContent Wizard when you are already working in PowerPoint, choose New from the File menu, click the Presentations tab, and then double-click the AutoContent Wizard icon.)

Wizards

Wizards are tools that are incorporated into most Microsoft applications to help you accomplish specific tasks. They work in the same basic way, regardless of the task or the application. Wizards consist of a series of dialog boxes that ask you to provide information or to select from various options. You move from box to box by clicking the Next button, and you can move back to an earlier box by clicking the Back button. Clicking Cancel aborts the entire procedure, and clicking Finish tells the wizard to complete the task with the current settings. Some wizards, such as the Auto-Content Wizard, include a "road map" with colored boxes representing the wizard's steps. You can see where you are in the process by glancing at the boxes, and you can jump to a particular step by clicking its box.

1. With the PowerPoint dialog box open on your screen, select the AutoContent Wizard option and then click OK to display the first of five AutoContent Wizard dialog boxes:

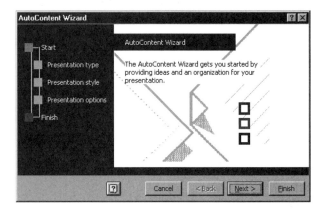

2. Read the information in the dialog box, and then click Next to move to this dialog box, where you select the type of presentation you want to create:

Adding and removing presentation types

If you use only a few presentation types but they are scattered across several categories, you can list them all in one category for convenience. Click the button for the category you want to contain your presentation types, and then click the Add button in the second AutoContent Wizard dialog box. In the Select Presentation Template dialog box, select the presentation type you want and click OK. To remove a presentation type from a category, just select it and then click Remove. PowerPoint warns you that if the type is no longer listed in at least one category, removing it will make it inaccessible via the Auto-Content Wizard.

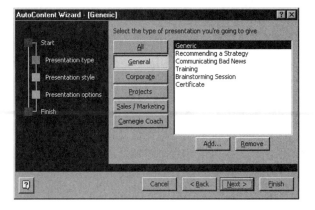

The "road map" on the left tells you to specify a presentation type. All the types are listed on the right, and the buttons in the middle allow you to display the types by category.

3. Click the buttons in the middle of the dialog box to see the presentation types in each category. When you're ready, click the Sales/Marketing button, select Marketing Plan, and then click Next to display the dialog box shown at the top of the facing page.

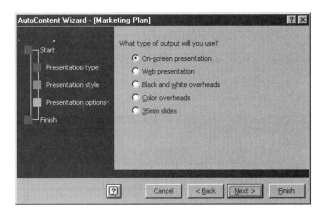

4. Check that On-Screen Presentation is selected as your output option, and click Next to display the dialog box shown here:

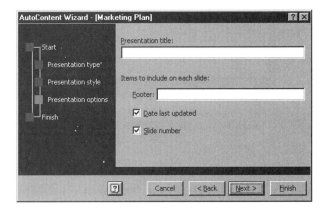

The information you enter in this dialog box will become the first slide, called the *title slide*, of the presentation.

5. In the Presentation Title edit box, type *Paranormal Tours*, and in the Footer edit box, type *Exotic Excursions*. Click Next to display the AutoContent Wizard's final dialog box:

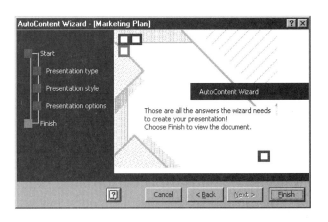

Different configurations

We wrote this book using a computer running Microsoft Windows 98 with the screen resolution set to 800x600. If you are using a different version of Windows or a different resolution, your screens won't match ours exactly. We were also using the PowerPoint configuration that results from a Typical installation of Microsoft Office 2000 from CD-ROM. If a system administrator installed PowerPoint for you, your setup may be different. However, you will still be able to follow along with most of the examples in this book.

6. Click Finish. PowerPoint opens a presentation window like the one shown below. (Don't worry that a different name appears in your presentation. We'll address that issue on page 13.)

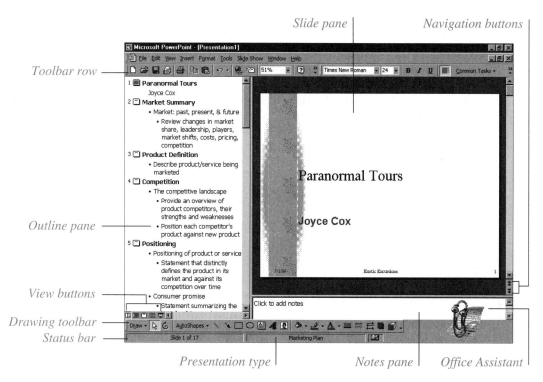

Slide pane *Navigation buttons*

Toolbar row

Outline pane

View buttons

Drawing toolbar

Status bar

Presentation type   *Notes pane*   *Office Assistant*

Normal view

Taking up most of the screen is your new presentation, which PowerPoint shows in *normal view* in the window's work area. In the left pane is an outline of your presentation. The first topic in the outline is the title-slide information you entered in the fourth AutoContent Wizard dialog box. The remaining topics are PowerPoint's suggestions for items you might want to cover in a marketing plan. In the top right pane is the slide that corresponds to the outline's first topic, displayed with the design template assigned to the marketing-plan presentation type. (See page 61 for more information about templates.) At the bottom of the slide pane's vertical scroll bar are the Previous Slide and Next Slide buttons, which you can click to move backward and forward through the presentation's slides. In the bottom right pane is an area where you can add notes.

The Previous Slide and Next Slide buttons

Like most Windows applications, the Microsoft PowerPoint window includes the familiar title bar at the top and a status bar at the bottom. You can also see the menu bar and toolbars.

Although the menu bar and toolbars look the same as those in all Windows applications, they work a little differently, so we'll take a moment to explore them here.

The *menu bar* changes to reflect the menus and commands for the presentation component you are working with. You use standard Windows techniques to choose a command from a menu or submenu and to work with dialog boxes. However, PowerPoint 2000 goes beyond the basic Windows procedure for choosing commands by determining which commands you are most likely to use and adjusting the display of commands on each menu to reflect how you use the program. As a quick example, let's take a look at the View menu:

Choosing commands

1. Click *View* on the menu bar to drop down the View menu. The two arrows at the bottom of the menu indicate that one or more commands are hidden because they are not the ones most people use most of the time.

2. Continue pointing to the word *View*. The two arrows disappear and more commands appear on the menu. (You can also click the two arrows to make hidden commands appear.) The status of a less frequently used command is indicated by a lighter shade of gray. If you choose one of the light gray commands, in the future it will appear in the same color as other commands and will no longer be hidden.

3. Move the pointer away from the menu bar and menu and press Esc twice to deactivate them both.

Another way to give PowerPoint an instruction is by clicking a button on a *toolbar*. This is the equivalent of choosing the corresponding command from a menu and if necessary, clicking OK to accept all the default settings in the command's dialog box. PowerPoint comes with many built-in toolbars, equipped with buttons that help you accomplish specific tasks. You will use some toolbars frequently, and others you may never use. By default, PowerPoint displays two of its most useful toolbars—the Standard and Formatting toolbars—on a single toolbar row below the menu bar. It overlaps the toolbars and, as with menus, initially displays only the most frequently used buttons on each toolbar. As shown

Shortcut menus

For efficiency, the commands you are likely to use with a particular element of a presentation (such as a bulleted list) or the presentation window (such as a toolbar) are grouped on special menus called *shortcut menus*. You can display an element's shortcut menu by pointing to the element and clicking the right mouse button. (This action is known as *right-clicking*.) In this book, we give instructions for choosing shortcut menu commands when that is the most efficient way of accomplishing a task.

The More Buttons button

here, each toolbar has a move handle at its left end and a More Buttons button at its right end, both of which allow you to display currently hidden buttons:

Standard toolbar | *More Buttons button* | *Formatting toolbar*

Move handles —

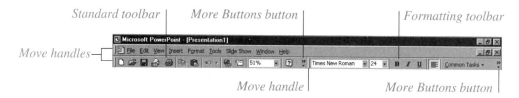

Move handle | *More Buttons button* |

Let's do some exploring:

ScreenTips

1. Point to each button on the toolbars. PowerPoint's *Screen-Tips* feature displays a box with the button's name.

2. Point to the Formatting toolbar's move handle, and when the pointer changes to a four-headed arrow, drag it to the right until only the Common Tasks button is visible, as shown here:

Standard toolbar | *Move handle* | *Formatting toolbar*

Move handles —

More Buttons button |

Personalized menus and toolbars

As you have seen, PowerPoint's menus and toolbars adjust themselves to the way you work, making more commands and buttons available as you use them. Commands and buttons you don't use are hidden so that they don't get in the way. As a result, your menus and toolbars may not look exactly like ours, and occasionally, we may tell you to choose a command or click a button that is not visible. When this happens, don't panic. Simply pull down the menu and wait for all its commands to be displayed, or click the toolbar's More Buttons button to display its hidden buttons.

3. Now click the Formatting toolbar's More Buttons button to see this palette of all the hidden buttons on that toolbar:

You'll work extensively with the buttons on these and other toolbars. For now, let's save the presentation on your screen.

Saving a Presentation

To save a new presentation, you can choose Save As from the File menu or click the Save button. Follow these steps:

1. Choose Save As from the File menu. The dialog box on the facing page is displayed so that you can name the presentation.

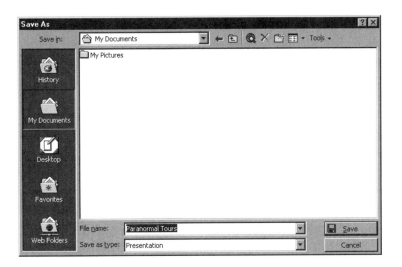

2. PowerPoint suggests the first few words in the presentation as its name in the File Name edit box. In this case, *Paranormal Tours* is what you want.

3. Be sure the My Documents folder appears in the Save In box, leave the other settings in the dialog box as they are, and click Save. When you return to the presentation, notice that *Paranormal Tours* has replaced *Presentation1* in the title bar.

   From now on, you can simply click the Save button or choose the Save command from the File menu any time you want to save changes to this presentation. Because PowerPoint knows the name of the presentation, it overwrites the previous version

The Save button

Saving options

When saving a presentation, you can change the file format by clicking the arrow to the right of the Save As Type edit box in the Save As dialog box and then selecting the format you want. Choose Options from the Tools menu and click the Save tab to display additional saving options. By default, the Allow Fast Saves, Save AutoRecover Info Every, and Convert Charts When Saving As Previous Version options are turned on. On the Save tab, you can turn them off or change the amount of time that goes by between fast saves. The Prompt For File Properties option tells PowerPoint to prompt for the file properties of a presentation when saving it. In the Save PowerPoint Files As edit box, you can specify the default file format used when saving a presentation. You can also specify a default folder for where your presentations are saved by entering the folder's path in the Default File Location edit box.

Saving in another folder

The presentation will be saved in the folder designated in the Save In box. To store a presentation in a different folder, click the arrow to the right of the Save In box and navigate to that folder before clicking the Save button. You can use the icons on the shortcuts bar along the left side of the Save As dialog box to get to common folders and recent files. To create a new folder, click the Create New Folder button and name the folder before you save the file.

Saving with a new name ────────►

with the new version. If you want to save your changes but preserve the previous version, you can assign a different name to the new version by choosing the Save As command from the File menu, entering the new name in the File Name edit box, and clicking Save.

Switching Views

In the bottom left corner of the work area is a row of buttons you can use to switch from one view of a presentation to another. Right now, the Normal View button appears "pressed" because you are in normal view. Let's move to *slide view*, where you can concentrate on the content of the presentation one slide at a time. Follow this quick step:

Slide view ────────►

The Slide View button ────────►

1. Click the Slide View button in the bottom left corner of the work area, or choose Slide from the View menu. Your screen now looks like this:

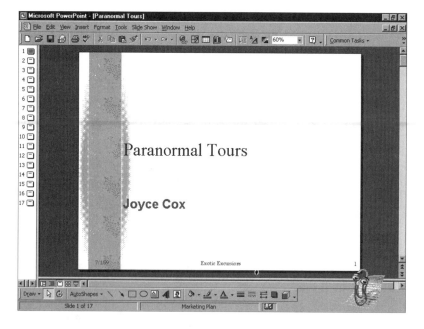

The outline pane has shrunk to display only the slide icons and numbers, with Slide 1—the title slide—selected. The notes pane has disappeared, and the slide pane now takes up most of the work area, with Slide 1 displayed.

Editing Slides

Now you're ready to customize the text of the slides created by the AutoContent Wizard, which you can do either on the slides or in the outline. In a strong presentation, each slide must stand on its own as well as contribute to the overall message you want to convey, so when you first start creating presentations, you will probably want to work in slide view to see how each slide looks. Once you have a few presentations under your belt, you might find it quicker to work in outline view and then switch to slide view to see the results. In either case, you can go back and make changes at any time, so don't worry about getting stuck with something less than perfect. In fact, it's often best to leave the fine-tuning until the end of the development process; too much fussing can bog down even a short project.

Editing Text

Let's edit the existing slides so that they provide details about the new Paranormal Tours line. You'll start with changing the name on the title slide. When PowerPoint created this slide, it assumed the presentation was being developed by the person whose name is assigned to your computer, and added that name below the presentation title. Follow these steps to change the name:

1. Click the existing name to select the area in which it appears on the slide, or click below the title if there is no name.

2. Using any standard Windows selection technique, select the name and then type *Ima Tripp*. (The red, wavy underline beneath *Ima* indicates a possible misspelling. We discuss spell-checking on page 69, so ignore the underline for now.)

Now you'll edit the bulleted and subordinate items on some of the other slides. Follow these steps:

1. Click the Next Slide button at the bottom of the vertical scroll bar to move to the second slide. As shown on the next page, this slide has a *title* (its topic), a *bulleted item*, a *subordinate item*, and a sample graph.

Changing your mind about an edit

If you make a mistake or change your mind while editing a slide, you can click the Undo button on the Standard toolbar to reverse your last action. To reinstate that action, simply click the Redo button. You can also undo and redo multiple actions at a time. Click the arrow to the right of the appropriate button and drag through the actions in the list that you want to undo or redo. You can't undo or redo a single action other than the last one (which is the first one in the list). For example, to undo the third action in the list, you must also undo the first and the second. You can change the number of actions you want PowerPoint to track in the Undo/Redo lists by choosing Options from the Tools menu, clicking the Edit tab, and changing the number in the Maximum Number Of Undos box.

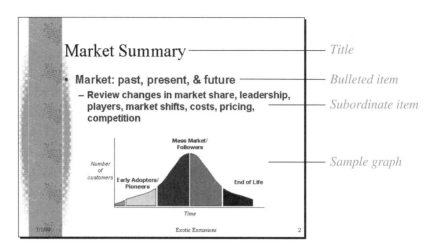

Title
Bulleted item
Subordinate item
Sample graph

The title area

2. Select the title text. (A shaded border surrounds the *title area*.) Type *Objectives*.

The object area

3. Select the bulleted item's text. (A shaded border surrounds the *object area*.) Then type *To provide new tour packages for affiliated agencies* (no period).

Adding items

4. Press Enter to create another bulleted item, and type *To satisfy the public's increasing interest in the paranormal* (no period). As you type, PowerPoint expands the object area to accommodate more items. When it can't expand the area any more, PowerPoint shrinks the font size so that everything fits.

Deleting items

5. Select the subordinate item's text and press Backspace until the insertion point is at the end of the previous bulleted item. The results are shown here:

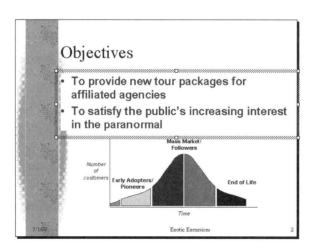

6. Click each object in the sample graph and press Delete to remove the object. (For the text boxes, click once and then click the surrounding frame once before pressing Delete.)

7. Save your changes. (Remember to save at regular intervals as you work. A good rule of thumb is to save anything you don't want to do over again.)

Slide 2 looks pretty good, so let's move on to the next slide and continue editing:

1. Click the icon for Slide 3 in the outline pane to display that slide. Then replace the title text with *Customer Requirements*.

2. Next replace the text of the bulleted item with *Tours that are not only insightful but enjoyable* (no period).

3. Press Enter to create a second bulleted item and type *Tours that focus on the latest developments in paranormalism* (again, no period).

4. Press Enter to create a third bulleted item and then type *Tour packages that are flexible* (no period). Here are the results:

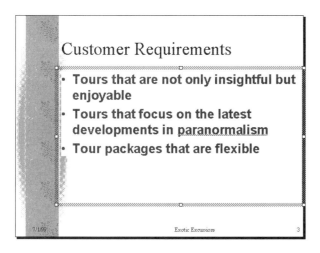

Now let's customize Slide 4:

1. Click the Next Slide button to move to Slide 4, and change the title to *Some Sample Tours*.

2. Replace the text of the first bulleted item with *Ghostly Bed and Breakfasts*.

The fewer bulleted items, the better

The more bullets on a slide, the harder it is for your audience to focus on any one of the points you are trying to make. You have a better chance of getting your message across to your audience if you limit the number of bulleted items to six lines. If you have many bulleted items, break them into logical groups and use a different slide for each group.

3. Next replace the text of the first subordinate item with *United States*. (Remember to leave out the periods as you type these entries.)

4. Select the text of the second subordinate item, type *Europe*, and press Enter to add a third subordinate item.

5. Change your mind and delete the word *Europe*.

Promoting and Demoting Items

Sometimes you will need to convert a bulleted item to a subordinate item, and vice versa. Follow these steps to see how to promote and demote items:

1. You want to convert the blank subordinate item on Slide 4 to a bulleted item. With the insertion point in the subordinate item, click the More Buttons button at the right end of the Formatting toolbar.

The Promote button

2. Click the Promote button on the More Buttons palette. Power-Point changes the bullet character and moves the line out to the margin. (It also makes the Promote button visible on the Formatting toolbar.)

3. Type *Mythical Monsters*.

4. Press Enter to create another bulleted item, and then type *Extraterrestrial Exploration*.

The Demote button

5. Now suppose you want to add another subordinate item after the first bulleted item. Click an insertion point to the right of the *s* in *Breakfasts* and press Enter to create a new bulleted item. Then click the Demote button on the Formatting toolbar's More Buttons palette. Type *Europe*.

6. Click the graph object on the right side of the slide and press Delete. Slide 4 now looks like the one shown at the top of the facing page.

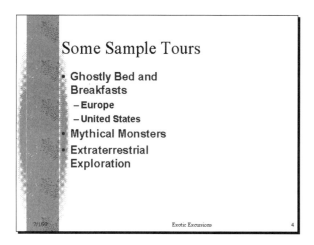

Let's quickly edit the text of the remaining slides of the Paranormal Tours presentation. As you follow the steps below, you'll notice misspelled words that appear in bold. Be sure to type the words exactly as they appear so that you have something to correct when you check your spelling in Chapter 3.

1. Click the Next Slide button to display Slide 5, and replace the title with *Customer **Sirvey.***

2. Next replace the first bulleted item with *Over the last **dekade**, public interest in paranormal phenomena has increased 40%.*

3. Select the remaining text on the slide and press Delete. Slide 5 now looks like this:

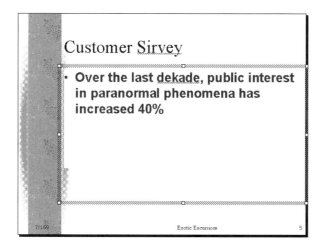

Five levels of bullets

In PowerPoint, you can create up to five levels of bulleted items on a slide, but we recommend that you use no more than two levels. Using more than two levels almost always results in crowded slides that are difficult to read and hard to understand.

4. Click the Next Slide button to display Slide 6, which will be the final slide in the Paranormal Tours presentation.

5. Replace the title with ***Rap*** *Up* and then replace the first bulleted item with *By endorsing the Paranormal Tours line, Exotic* ***Excrusions*** *Incorporated will be at the* ***forfront*** *of worldwide travel agencies.* Delete the remaining text on the slide. Now the slide looks like this:

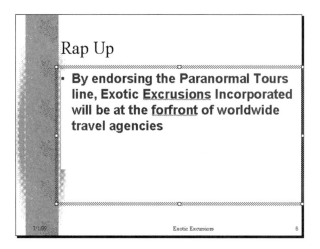

Deleting Slides

You've completed the "first draft" of the Paranormal Tours presentation, but you still need to get rid of the extraneous slides created by the AutoContent Wizard. Deleting slides is easy to accomplish in outline view, so let's switch to that view and delete the 11 remaining slides of the presentation. Follow these steps:

The Outline View button

1. Click the Outline View button in the bottom left corner of the window or choose Outline from the View menu. Your screen looks similar to the one shown on page 8 except that, as you can see, the outline pane now occupies most of the work area, and the active slide is displayed in a small slide pane.

Selecting multiple slides

2. Click the Slide 7 icon to select it, scroll the outline pane until you can see Slide 17, hold down the Shift key, and click the Slide 17 icon. The last 11 slides are now selected.

3. Press Delete to delete all the selected slides, and then click OK to confirm the deletion.

4. Press Ctrl+Home to move to the first slide.

5. Click the Save button to safeguard your work.

Adding Special Effects

If you will use your PowerPoint presentation to create 35mm slides or overhead transparencies, the only movement in your presentation will be the change from one slide to the next, and the only sound will probably be that of your own voice. If you will use your presentation as an electronic slide show, you have the potential for introducing dynamic special effects.

In this section, we'll briefly look at PowerPoint's built-in animation and sound effects to give you a taste of how you can quickly add pizazz to your presentations. Try this:

1. Switch to slide view. With the title slide on your screen, click the Formatting toolbar's More Buttons button and then click the Animation Effects button to display its toolbar.

The Animation Effects button

2. Click the slide's title to select it. Now all the buttons on the Animation Effects toolbar are available.

3. Click the Drive-In Effect button.

The Drive-In Effect button

4. Choose Animation Preview from the expanded Slide Show menu to display a preview window. Then arrange the Animation Effects toolbar and the window like this:

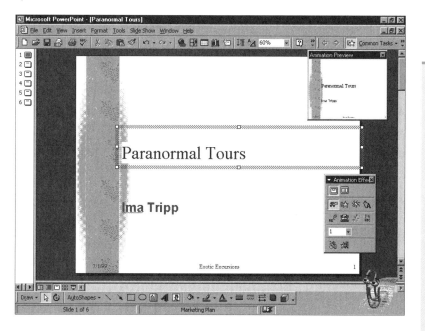

Install on demand

If you attempt to use a feature that is not installed, PowerPoint asks whether you want to install it. Insert the installation CD-ROM and click Yes. PowerPoint then starts the installation process. When the installation is complete, Power-Point loads the specified feature or starts the appropriate wizard. This install on demand capability allows you to install items as you need them rather than having to store several items on your hard drive that you may never need to use.

The Animate Title button

5. Click anywhere in the preview window to see the animation and hear the sound associated with the drive-in effect. (Notice that the Animate Title button on the Animation Effects toolbar is now turned on. If you change your mind about applying an animation effect, you can click this button to restore the title to its former unanimated state.)

6. Click each of the buttons on the Animation Effects toolbar in turn, previewing their animation and sounds in the preview window. When you're through exploring, finish up with the drive-in effect.

7. Next click the name on the title slide to select its object area.

The Reverse Text Order Effect button

8. Click the Reverse Text Order Effect button and then click the preview window to see the effects applied to both the name Ima Tripp and the title.

Now let's look at an animation effect that builds a bulleted list. Follow these steps:

1. Move to Slide 2, select the title area, click the Animate Title button, and then preview the default animation effect by clicking the Animation Preview button.

The Animation Preview button

2. You want the titles of each of your slides to have the same effect, so click the Drive-In Effect button and preview again.

3. Now select Slide 2's object area by clicking anywhere in the bulleted list.

4. Again click each animation button in turn and preview the effect on the bulleted list by simply clicking the preview window. (Notice that the Animate Slide Text button is now turned on.)

The Animate Slide Text button

The Flying Effect button

5. Finish by clicking the Flying Effect button.

Well, as you probably noticed, effects that are suitable for titles are not necessarily suitable for bulleted lists. In fact, the effect you have selected is somewhat jarring for more than a couple of words of text, because your eyes are accustomed to reading from left to right, not right to left. If none of the built-in effects is quite what you want, you can always create a custom effect by following these steps:

1. Select the object area, click the Custom Animation button, and click the Order & Timing tab to see these options:

The Custom Animation button

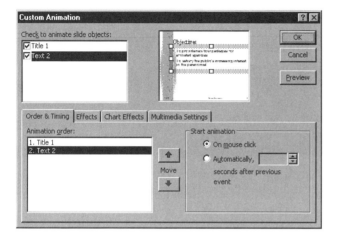

The settings in the Start Animation section for the item selected in the Animation Order list tell you that the bulleted items will appear when you click the mouse button. You can also specify that the items should appear automatically after a certain number of seconds.

2. Click the Effects tab to display these options:

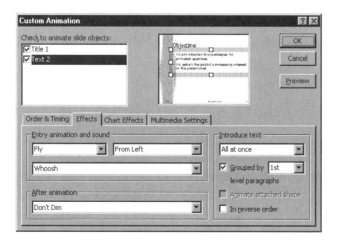

Changing the animation order

As you animate areas or objects, they are assigned a number in the edit box on the Animation Effects toolbar. You can change the order of the animations by changing the assigned numbers. For example, you can select the object area and change its number in the edit box to 1 and then select the title area and change its number to 2. The object area animation will then start first, and the title area animation will follow.

The settings on this tab are those that PowerPoint assigns to the Flying Effect button.

3. Leave the Fly setting as it is, but click the arrow to the right of the second edit box in the Entry Animation And Sound section and select From Bottom-Left.

4. Click the arrow to the right of the top edit box in the Introduce Text section and select By Word.

5. Click the Preview button to see the effects of your changes, and then experiment with other effects so that you know what is available.

6. Finish up with Fly, From Top-Right, and All At Once as the selections, but don't click OK yet.

To keep your audience's attention focused on your current point, you can dim or hide the bullets you have already shown by following these steps:

Dimming or hiding displayed bulleted items

1. Click the arrow to the right of the edit box in the After Animation section and select the fifth color from the left (pale blue).

2. Preview this effect, noticing how PowerPoint changes the color of the displayed items as it brings in a new item.

3. Click OK to close the Custom Animation dialog box and implement your settings, which you can preview again by clicking the preview window.

4. If you want, experiment with applying animation effects to the remaining slides of the presentation. Then close the preview window and the Animation Effects toolbar by clicking their Close buttons.

Viewing a Presentation

Whether you are going to output your presentation as slides or transparencies or deliver it as an electronic slide show, you will want to view it first on your computer to check what your audience will see. Let's view the presentation:

Adding sound effects

If your computer can produce sound, you can add this effect to your presentation. Click the Custom Animation button and on the Animation Effects toolbar, select the sound you want to apply to the selected object. If you have a microphone, you may want to record your own, or you can use sounds from another source. Then to use the effect, select Other Sounds from the sounds drop-down list, navigate to the sound file, and double-click it.

The Slide Show button

1. Move to Slide 1, and then click the Slide Show button in the bottom left corner of the work area to display the first slide of the presentation in slide show view.

2. Without moving the mouse, click the left mouse button to display the title. Then click again to display the presenter's name. The slide now looks like this:

3. To move to the next slide, click the left mouse button or press the PageDown key. The title flies in from the right.

4. Click or press PageDown to bring in each of the bulleted items.

5. Continue clicking the left mouse button to step through the slides one at a time. To move to the previous slide, press the PageUp key. (You can also click the right mouse button and choose Previous from the shortcut menu. However, when delivering your presentation to an audience, having a shortcut menu appear on the screen might interrupt the flow and effect of the slide show.) You can cancel the slide show at any time by pressing Esc.

6. When you reach the last slide (Rap Up), click the left mouse button again. PowerPoint displays a black slide announcing the end of the show.

Slide show tools

If you move the mouse pointer across a slide while in slide show view, a button appears in the bottom left corner of your screen. You can click this button to display a menu of helpful slide show tools. (This menu also appears if you click the right mouse button.) If you move the mouse by mistake, don't worry. The button will disappear when you click the left mouse button to move on to the next slide.

7. Click again to switch back to the view you were in before you clicked the Slide Show button.

You now know how to create simple presentations and view them on your computer. In the next chapters, we'll look at how to embellish your presentations for maximum impact. But in the meantime, let's take a brief tour of PowerPoint's Help feature.

Getting Help

This tour of PowerPoint has covered a lot of ground in just a few pages, and you might be wondering how you will manage to retain it all. Don't worry. If you forget how to carry out a particular task, help is never far away. You've already seen how the ScreenTips feature can jog your memory about the functions of the toolbar buttons. And you may have noticed that the dialog boxes contain a Help button (the question mark), which you can click to get information about their options. Here, you'll look at ways to get information using the Office Assistant. Follow these steps:

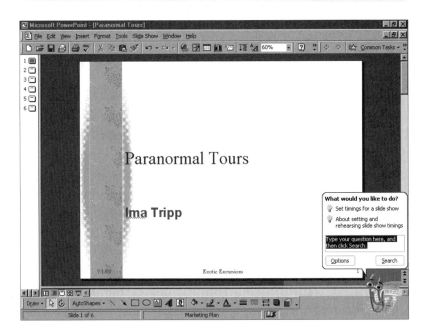

The Microsoft PowerPoint Help button

1. Click the Office Assistant or click the Microsoft PowerPoint Help button on the Standard toolbar to display a message box like this one:

You can type a question in the Search box and then click the Search button to have the Office Assistant search for topics that most closely match your question.

2. Type *Add animation* and click the Search button. The Office Assistant displays a list of topics related to your question.

3. Click the *Animate text and objects* topic. The Office Assistant moves out of the way so that you can see the Help window shown below. (It may take a few seconds to prepare the Help file for its first use.)

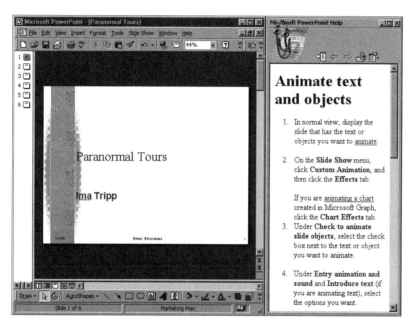

More about the Office Assistant

If the Office Assistant displays a light bulb above its icon, it has a tip for you. Click the light bulb to see the tip. To move the Office Assistant to another location on the screen, you can simply drag it. To display the search box, click the Office Assistant. If having the assistant on the screen bothers you, or if you would like to custo-mize it, click the Office Assis-tant's Options button to open the Office Assistant dialog box. Here, you can select and deselect vari-ous options that control when the Office Assistant appears, whether it makes sounds, and what tips it displays. To turn off the Office Assistant permanently, deselect the Use The Office Assistant check box. (If you want the assis-tant to temporarily disappear or reappear, choose Hide/ Show The Office Assistant from the Help menu.) On the Gallery tab, you can click the Back or Next button to scroll through the different ani-mated characters for the assistant (the default is the paper clip) and then click OK to change the assis-tant. (You may need to insert your installation CD-ROM to complete the switch.)

As you can see, the Help window appears on the right side of the screen so that you can follow the instructions in your pre-sentation.

If you prefer to get help without the asking the Office Assis-tant a question, you can use the Index tab of the Help window. Follow these steps:

1. Click the Show button (the one with the left pointing arrow) at the top of the Help window and then click the Index tab to dis-play the options shown on the next page.

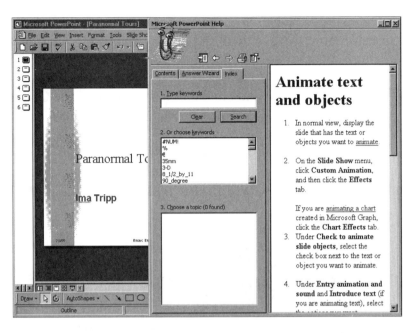

2. In the Type Keywords box, type *anim*. The list below scrolls to display topics beginning with the letters you type, and the Type Keywords entry changes to the first available topic.

3. With *animation* selected in the Or Choose Keywords list box, click the Search button. Then click *Preview animation in a slide* in the Choose A Topic list to display the information in the right pane.

4. Click the Help window's Close button.

We'll leave you to explore other Help topics on your own.

Using Contents

The Contents tab of the Help window organizes topics into categories that are represented by book icons. You can display a category's topics by clicking its plus sign. More book icons may appear, representing subcategories. You can click a topic (designated by a question mark icon) to display its information in the right pane of the Help window.

Using the Answer Wizard

The Answer Wizard provides a way to type search questions without the Office Assistant interface. To access the Answer Wizard, display the Help window, click the Answer Wizard tab, type a question in the edit box, and then click Search. PowerPoint displays a list of topics that most closely fit your question. You can click a topic to display its contents in the pane on the right.

Using the Web

If you have a modem and are connected to the Internet, you can access the Microsoft Office Update Web site as well as other Microsoft Web sites to get information or technical support. Choose Office On The Web from the Help menu to start your Web browser, connect to the Internet, and display the Microsoft Office Update Web site.

Quitting PowerPoint

You have seen how to use PowerPoint to create a simple text-based presentation. Easy, wasn't it? All that's left is to show you how to end a PowerPoint session. Follow these steps:

1. Choose Exit from the File menu.

2. If the Office Assistant asks whether you want to save the changes you have made to the open presentation, click Yes.

Here are some other ways to quit PowerPoint:

- Click the Close button at the right end of PowerPoint's title bar.

- Press Alt, then F (the underlined letter in *File* on the menu bar), then X (the underlined letter in *Exit* on the File menu).

- Double-click the Control menu icon—the small slide next to the words *Microsoft PowerPoint*—at the left end of Power-Point's title bar.

You have covered a lot of ground and are now up to speed on the basic steps involved in creating a presentation. As you work your way through the next chapters, you'll build on your PowerPoint skills and learn more ways to enhance your presentations.

Presenting Information Visually

This chapter shows how to add visual appeal to your presentations. You add clip art from the Microsoft Clip Gallery, import a graphic from a different source, and then add animation to it. You finish by adding and formatting a graph using Microsoft Graph.

As you continue to work with the presentation for the new tour line, you'll undoubtedly begin to think of ways to use the techniques you learn in this chapter in other types of presentations, such as product demonstrations or market surveys.

Presentation created and concepts covered:

Import graphics and add them to the Clip Gallery for easy access

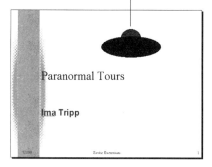

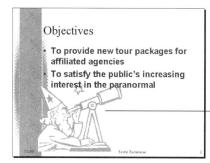

Crop away parts you don't want and then place in the background

Change the format of a slide so that you can add a graph

Add a graphic from the Clip Gallery and then size and position it

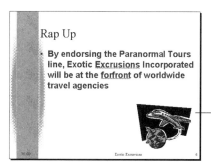

The Clip Gallery

Words are great, but words alone won't always get your message across. Fortunately, you can easily add visual elements to your slides to illustrate a point or spruce up your presentation. As you'll see, you can use the pictures in the Clip Gallery to dress up your slides, and with hundreds of pictures to choose from, the Clip Gallery has a picture to fit just about any need. Or if you need to present facts or figures in a visual format that promotes at-a-glance understanding of trends or relationships, you can include a graph to show important changes in data.

In this chapter, we first show you how to enhance your presentations by adding clip art graphics to slides. You learn how to size and manipulate the graphics, how to import graphics from other sources, and how to animate graphics. Then we show you how to add and fine-tune a graph. Before you can get going, you need to open your existing presentation. You could accomplish this task by clicking the Start button and choosing Paranormal Tours from the Documents submenu, but let's take the scenic route. Follow these steps:

Opening an existing document

1. Start PowerPoint by choosing it from the Programs submenu of the Start menu. PowerPoint displays the dialog box shown earlier on page 5.

2. Click the Open An Existing Presentation option. PowerPoint activates the list below, which includes the presentation you worked on in Chapter 1.

3. Double-click My Documents\Paranormal Tours to open it in the presentation window.

4. When PowerPoint opens an existing presentation, it displays the presentation's first slide in slide view. In the next section, you want to work with the last slide, Slide 6, so click the Slide 6 icon in the outline pane to display the Rap Up slide shown on the facing page. (We've hidden the Office Assistant by choosing Hide The Office Assistant from the Help menu. If you want to work without its help, you can do the same.) Now you're ready to learn about graphics.

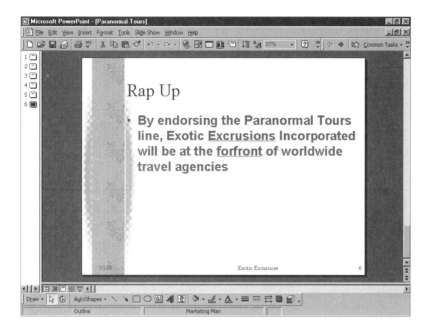

Adding Clip Art to Slides

You can add clip art to an existing slide or create a new slide with a clip art placeholder. In this next section, we'll show you how to add clip art to an existing slide in the Paranormal Tours presentation now on your screen. (For information about creating new slides with clip art, see the tip on the next page.)

When PowerPoint was installed on your computer, most likely not all of the available clip art was copied to your hard disk. Several other files can be viewed and imported into a presentation from PowerPoint's installation CD-ROM. In our examples, we use graphics that should be available without the CD-ROM. If you cannot access them, substitute any of the graphics that are available to you. Let's get started:

1. Click the Insert Clip Art button on the Drawing toolbar, which is docked at the bottom of your screen. Or choose Picture and then Clip Art from the Insert menu. PowerPoint displays the Clip Gallery window shown on the following page. Because you want to insert a graphic, the Clip Gallery's title bar reads *Insert ClipArt*. When you are inserting a sound or video file, the title bar changes accordingly.

The Insert Clip Art button

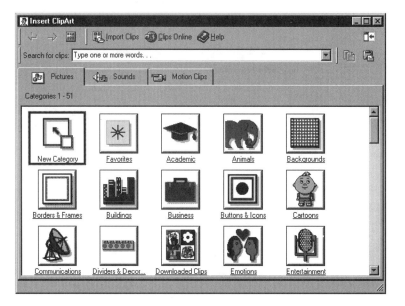

2. Click any category on the Pictures tab to see the clips available in that category. To return to the category list, click the Back button. (Some of the categories are empty so that you can fill them with clips that you download from Microsoft's Clip Gallery Web page, or from other Web sites.)

The Back button

3. When you finish browsing, click the Travel category, scroll through its clips, and then click the first clip. A palette of buttons appears. These buttons let you insert the clip, preview it, add it to the Favorites category or another category on the Pictures tab, or find similar clips.

The Insert Clip button

4. Click the Insert Clip button to add the graphic to Slide 6, and then close the Clip Gallery window. Here are the results:

Adding new clip art slides

You may want to create a brand new clip art slide, rather than add a clip art graphic to an existing slide. Simply click the New Slide button on the Standard toolbar and select one of the clip art autolayouts in the New Slide dialog box.

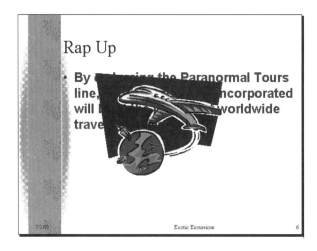

5. Save the presentation. (We won't tell you to save from now on, but you should remember to save often.)

Sizing and Positioning Clip Art

As with other objects in PowerPoint, you can easily resize and relocate clip art graphics on a slide. To change the size and location of the globe graphic, follow these steps:

1. If necessary, click the graphic to select it. PowerPoint surrounds the graphic with handles and displays the floating Picture toolbar.

2. Double-click the toolbar's title bar to "dock" it along the edge of the work area. The slide size decreases slightly to make room for the toolbar.

3. Point to one of the graphic's bottom corner handles. When the pointer changes to a double-headed arrow, hold down the left mouse button and drag upward until the graphic is about half its original size.

4. Next point anywhere inside the graphic. Hold down the left mouse button and drag downward and to the right until the graphic no longer obscures the text of the bulleted item and sits in the bottom right corner of the slide.

5. Click outside the graphic to deselect it. PowerPoint hides the Picture toolbar, and Slide 6 now looks something like the one shown here:

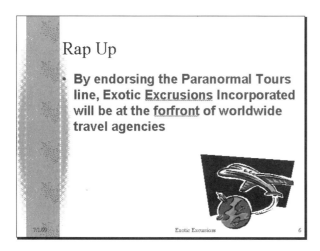

Adding autoshapes

You can use the Drawing toolbar's AutoShapes button to add shapes to your slides. For example, you can add a star by clicking the AutoShapes button, choosing Stars And Banners from the menu, and selecting the shape you want from the palette of options. Next position the mouse pointer on the slide, hold down the left mouse button, and drag the shape into place. You can resize the shape by dragging its handles, or reposition it by dragging it to a new location. If the autoshape has a diamond-shaped adjustment handle, you can drag the handle to adjust the shape's most prominent characteristic. (For example, you can change the angle of an isosceles triangle by dragging its adjustment handle.) To quickly replace an autoshape with another, select the shape, click the Draw button on the Drawing toolbar, choose Change AutoShape, and select a different shape from the drop-down palette of options.

Changing Clip Art Colors

If you like a clip art graphic's design but not its color scheme, you can change the set of colors assigned to it. Follow these steps to recolor the globe graphic:

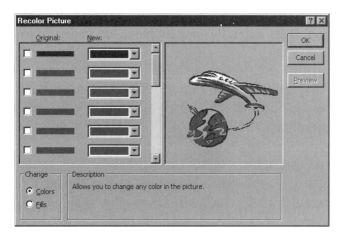

The Recolor Picture button

1. Select the graphic and click the Recolor Picture button on the Picture toolbar. You see this dialog box:

By default, the Colors option is selected in the Change section of the dialog box so that you can easily change any of the clip art graphic's colors. To change the graphic's background colors, you would select the Fills option.

Changing a graphic's background colors

2. Click the fourth check box in the Original section (light green), click the arrow to the right of the adjacent box in the New section to drop down a color palette, and select a different color.

3. Move the dialog box to the left by dragging its title bar, and then click Preview to see the how the graphic looks with the new color applied.

Adding borders to graphics

To add a border to any graphic object, select the object, and click the Format Picture button on the Picture toolbar. On the Colors And Lines tab of the Format Picture dialog box, change the Color setting in the Line section to the desired color, select a style and weight for the border, and click OK.

By default, the drop-down palette presents you with the eight colors of the presentation template's color scheme. (We talk more about templates on page 61.) If you want to use a different color, you can click the More Colors option to display the Colors dialog box, and then select from the Colors palette; or you can click the Custom tab to create a custom color. But if you use the predefined color scheme, your selection will co-ordinate with the other colors on the slide, and if you decide to change the entire color scheme, the colors of the graphic will then change accordingly.

4. Continue experimenting with other colors. When you achieve the desired effect, click OK. (We changed the fourth box to pale green and the ninth box from pale blue to bright blue.)

Searching for Clip Art

When you first opened the Clip Gallery, you might have noticed the Search For Clips edit box. Rather than scroll through the hundreds of graphics in the Gallery, you can use this box to locate a specific clip art graphic. Let's find an astronomer graphic and insert it on Slide 2 of Paranormal Tours by following the steps below:

1. Move to Slide 2 of the Paranormal Tours presentation.

2. Click the Insert Clip Art button on the Drawing toolbar, and when the Clip Gallery window appears, type *astronomers* in the Search For Clips edit box. Then press Enter. As you can see here, any graphic that relates to *astronomers* is now displayed in the Gallery:

                      Using keywords

3. Select the brown astronomer graphic in the first row, insert it, and close the Clip Gallery window. (Don't worry if the graphic obscures the bulleted text; you'll fix that later.)

Clip art keywords

All the graphics in the Clip Gallery window have been assigned keywords that describe their contents. If you point to a graphic and pause, these keywords appear in a pop-up box. To find a particular graphic, you can enter as many keywords as you want, separating them with commas.

If the results of a search don't identify a graphic you can use, you can always return to the Clip Gallery window and enter a different word in the Search For Clips edit box.

Cropping Clip Art

If you don't want to use all of a graphic, you can cut away the parts you don't want by *cropping* the image. (A cropped graphic can easily be restored to its original condition by clicking the Reset Picture button on the Picture toolbar.) In this section, we show you how to crop the astronomer graphic. But before we do, let's resize it:

The Reset Picture button

The Crop button

1. With Slide 2 displayed in slide view and the graphic selected, drag a bottom corner handle until the graphic has approximately tripled in size.

2. Click the Crop button on the Picture toolbar to activate the cropping tool.

3. Place the cropping tool over the bottom middle handle of the graphic and drag upward until the table is hidden. Then crop the left side of the astronomer in the same manner, so that the graphic looks like this:

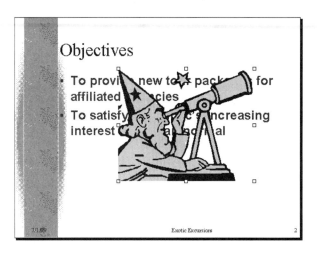

4. Click the Crop button again to deactivate the cropping tool.

5. Drag the cropped graphic to the left side of the slide and if necessary, resize it so that it looks as shown on the facing page.

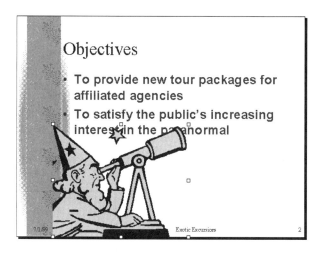

Adding Clip Art to the Background

You can add a clip art graphic to the background of a slide by following these steps:

1. With the graphic on Slide 2 selected, click the Draw button on the Drawing toolbar to display a menu of options.

2. Choose Order and then Send To Back from the pop-up menu. The bulleted item now overlays the graphic.

   You need to make the text of the bulleted item more legible, so let's do some recoloring:

1. Click the Recolor Picture button on the Picture toolbar to display its dialog box.

2. Click the second Original check box (brown), click the arrow to the right of the adjacent New box, and select the fifth of the eight color-scheme colors (sky blue). Then click the third

---

Creating graphics with PhotoDraw

Microsoft PhotoDraw 2000 is a powerful new graphics creation and manipulation program that is available with some editions of Office 2000 or as a stand-alone application. You can draw new graphics from scratch or using templates and shapes that come with the program. Or you can modify existing graphics with special effects that you apply in layers until the original is barely recognizable. You can even surround graphics with outlines of various shapes. PhotoDraw comes with a huge supply of graphics to choose from, or you can use its capabilities to "doctor" your own graphics. With all the permutations and combinations available, the possibilities are virtually unlimited.

original check box (beige) and change the adjacent New box to the first color (white) from the color scheme.

3. Check the preview box to see the changes before you apply them, and then click OK to see what Slide 4 looks like now:

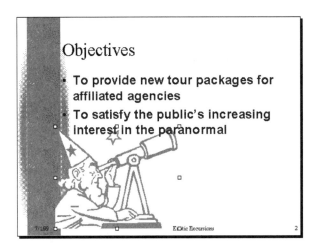

Importing Graphics

PowerPoint can import many graphics file formats, as long as you have installed the proper filters. (If Word or Excel is installed on your computer, PowerPoint can share their filters.) Here are the graphics file formats you can import:

Graphics file formats

Graphics file format	Extension
Computer Graphics Metafile	.CGM
CorelDRAW	.CDR
Encapsulated PostScript	.EPS
Enhanced Metafile	.EMF
FlashPix	.FPX
Graphics Interchange Format	.GIF
Hanako	.JSH, .JAH, .JBH
Joint Photographics Experts Group	.JPG
Kodak Photo CD	.PCD
Macintosh PICT	.PCT
PC Paintbrush	.PCX
Portable Network Graphics	.PNG
Tagged Image File Format	.TIF
Windows Bitmap	.BMP, .RLE, .DIB
Windows Metafile	.WMF
WordPerfect Graphics	.WPG

Adding a background graphic to all slides

To add a graphic to the background of all the slides in a presentation, first insert the graphic on the presentation's slide master, which controls the formatting of the presentation's slides. (For more information about masters, see page 119.) Then choose Order and Send To Back from the Draw button's menu.

To demonstrate just how easy it is to pull in a graphic from another source, we used the Windows Paint program to create a simple graphic called Ufo.bmp so that we could insert it on Slide 1 of Paranormal Tours. If you have a graphics file handy (anything will do), follow along now:

1. Move to Slide 1 and choose Picture and then From File from the Insert menu. The Insert Picture dialog box appears:

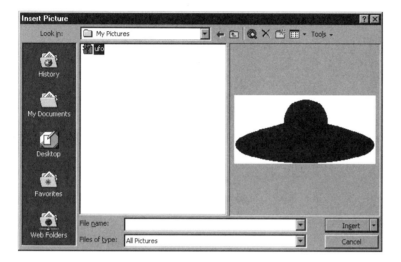

2. If you know the graphic's format, you can select it from the Files Of Type drop-down list. Then if necessary, move to the folder where the graphics file is located.

3. Double-click the graphics file (Ufo.bmp, in our case) in the list box to insert the graphic on the current slide, like this:

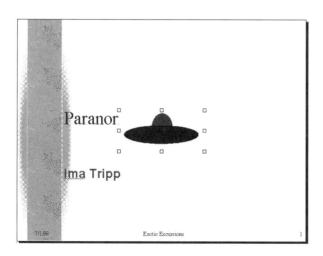

Importing graphics from the Web

If you have access to the Internet, you can import the graphics you download from Web sites into your presentations by following the steps above. (However, be sure anything you download is virus-free before you use it.) If yours is a commercial presentation and the graphics you want to use are copyrighted, be sure you obtain permission from the copyright holder to avoid any legal complications.

4. Now resize the graphic to an appropriate size, and drag it to the top right corner of the slide so that it sits directly above the word *Tours*.

The Set Transparent Color button

5. If the background of the graphic, but not the graphic itself, obscures the word *Tours*, click the Set Transparent Color button on the Picture toolbar. Then click the background of the graphic so that the slide's background shows through. The results are shown here:

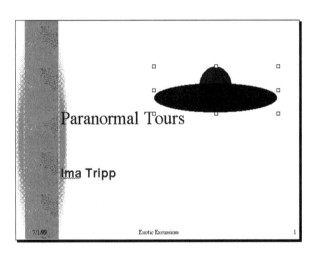

You can use the techniques described earlier to add an imported graphic to the slide's background. You can also recolor some types of imported graphics by using the methods you learned earlier in this chapter.

Adding Graphics to the Clip Gallery

If you want graphics from other applications to be as readily available as the clip art that came with PowerPoint, you can add the graphics to the Clip Gallery. Follow the steps below. (Again, we'll use Ufo.bmp as an example.)

1. Click the Insert Clip Art button on the Drawing toolbar to open the Clip Gallery window. Then click the Import Clips button to display the dialog box shown at the top of the facing page.

Scanned images

As with graphics files, you can easily import scanned images into your PowerPoint presentations. In slide view, first display the slide where you want to place the image and then choose Picture and From File from the Insert menu. Then in the Insert Picture dialog box, select the file containing the scanned image and click Insert. You can then crop, move, and resize the image like any other imported graphic. (If you don't have a scanner at your disposal, you can always take photographs or other images to a copy center or photo lab to have them scanned.)

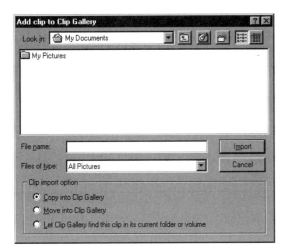

2. Navigate to the folder where the file is located, and double-click the graphic's filename. PowerPoint imports the file and then displays the Clip Properties dialog box, where a picture of the graphic appears in the top right corner:

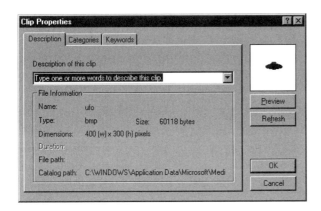

3. Next type a description in the Description edit box. (We entered *Unidentified flying object.*)

4. Click the Keywords tab. Then click the New Keyword button, type a word that you associate with your graphic, and click OK. Repeat this step for other keywords. (We entered *flying saucers, UFOs,* and *extraterrestrial.*)

Specifying keywords

5. Click the Categories tab, select a category name in the categories list, or click the New Category button, enter a new name, and click OK. (We entered the name *Paranormal.*) Then click OK again to close the Clip Properties dialog box and add the graphic to the Clip Gallery. (If the graphic is large, Power-Point may take a few minutes to add it to the Clip Gallery.)

Adding categories

6. Click Close to leave the Gallery.

Now whenever you want to insert this graphic, you can simply click the Insert Clip Art button and select the graphic from the Pictures tab of the Clip Gallery window.

Animating Graphics

In Chapter 1, you added animation effects to the text of some of your slides. Let's experiment further with animation by making the graphic you just added to the Gallery "fly" onto Slide 1. Follow these steps:

1. If necessary, click the graphic to select it. Then, from the Slide Show menu, choose Custom Animation to display the Custom Animation dialog box shown earlier on page 21.

2. Click the Order And Timing tab. In the Check To Animate Slide Objects box, click the Picture Frame 3 check box. PowerPoint moves the selection to the Animation Order box.

3. In the Start Animation section, click the Automatically option (but do not set a time).

4. Next click the Effects tab and then select the Fly and From Bottom-Left animation options. (If you have a sound card, you can select a sound option as well; we used Drive By.) Then click OK.

5. Click the Slide Show button and test the animation by clicking the mouse button until the graphic appears. Then press Esc to return to slide view.

Adding Graphs

Microsoft Graph

When it comes to presenting numerical data in a clear, concise way, nothing beats a graph. You can use graphs to depict a wide variety of information, from fluctuations in the weather to the value of a stock portfolio. In this section, we show you the ins and outs of using PowerPoint's built-in graphing program, Microsoft Graph. (By the way, in the following sections the terms *graph* and *chart* are used interchangeably.)

Using a Graph AutoLayout

You have several options for including a graph in a presentation. You can create a new slide that includes a placeholder, you can click the Insert Chart button on the Standard toolbar, or you can choose Microsoft Graph from the Insert menu. For this example, you'll change the layout of an existing slide of the Paranormal Tours presentation so that it will accommodate both its current text and a graph. Try this:

1. Move to Slide 5, right-click a blank area of the slide, and choose Slide Layout from the shortcut menu to display the dialog box shown below. (You can also click the Common Tasks button on the Formatting toolbar and select Slide Layout from the drop-down list.)

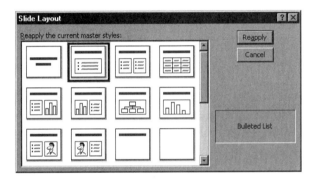

2. Select the Text & Chart Autolayout (the first autolayout in the second row) and click Apply. Slide 5 now looks like this:

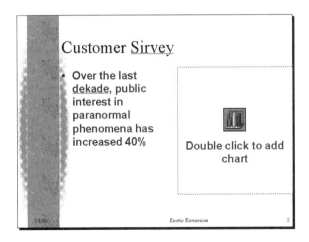

Customizing AutoContent Wizard graphs

The graphs displayed in the default Marketing Plan presentation created by the AutoContent Wizard (see page 5) are not true graphs. You cannot double-click them to start Graph. However, if you want to use these graphic "graphs," you can make minor changes to the text labels.

3. Double-click the graph placeholder to start Microsoft Graph. Your screen looks something like this:

Graph's menu bar ——

Graph's toolbars ——

Datasheet with placeholder data ——

Column chart of placeholder data ——

Graph displays a *datasheet* containing placeholder data, which resembles a worksheet in a spreadsheet program. In the left-most column and topmost row of the datasheet are gray headers that identify the columns by letter and the rows by number. Depending on whether your data is organized by row or by column (see the adjacent tip), one set of headers also displays icons that indicate the current chart type. (The default is a three-dimensional column chart.)

On the white part of the datasheet, you enter the data you want to plot. Gridlines divide the datasheet into units called *cells*. The first column and first row are reserved for headings called *labels*, which are used to identify information on the graph. You enter data by first clicking a cell to select it and then typing the information. To move to another cell, you can click it with the mouse; use the Arrow keys; or press Enter (to move to the cell below); Shift+Enter (to move to the cell above); Tab (to move to the next cell); or Shift+Tab (to move to the previous cell). You can press Home or End to move to the beginning or end of the current row, or Ctrl+Home or Ctrl+End to move to the beginning or end of the datasheet.

By row or by column

You can arrange the data series in a datasheet by row or by column. By default, Graph plots the series by row. But if you arrange the series by column, you can ensure that Graph will plot your data correctly by clicking the By Column button on Graph's Standard toolbar. If you want to return to the by row arrangement, simply click the By Row button. Graph puts miniature markers on the row number buttons of the datasheet if the data series will be plotted by row and on the column letter buttons if the data series will be plotted by column.

Now that you're acquainted with Graph's datasheet, let's replace its placeholder data with your own information, starting with the labels:

1. Click the 1st Qtr label in column A. (If you click outside the datasheet or graph, you will return to PowerPoint. Double-click the graph on the current slide to start Graph again.)

2. Type *1989*, press Tab to move to column B, and type *1999*.

3. Click the East label in row 1.

4. Type *Eastern*, press Enter to move to row 2, and type *Central*.

5. Press Enter one more time and type *Western*.

To speed up the entry of the remaining data in the datasheet, try this technique:

1. Point to the second cell in column A, hold down the left mouse button, drag to the fourth cell in column B, and then release the mouse button. The datasheet should look like this:

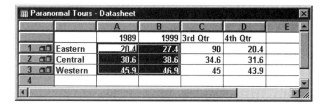

2. In column A type *20%*, press Enter, type *22%*, press Enter, type *25%*, and press Enter. In column B, type *29%*, *31%*, and

Adjusting column width

To increase or decrease the width of a column in a datasheet, first select the column. (To select an entire column or row, simply click the corresponding header button. To select the entire datasheet, click the "blank" button located at the intersection of the column letter and row number buttons.) Choose Column Width from Graph's Format menu and enter a number in the Column Width dialog box. Click the Best Fit button in the Column Width dialog box to automatically adjust the column width to fit the longest entry in the column. You can also use the mouse to change the column width. Point to the border that separates adjacent column letter buttons. When the pointer changes to a two-headed arrow, hold down the left mouse button and then drag to the right or left. If you double-click the border between two column letter buttons, the width of the column on the left is automatically adjusted to fit the longest entry. You can select multiple columns and use any of the methods described above to change the width of all the selected columns simultaneously.

38%, pressing Enter after each number. (By the way, this data is fictitious and is used for demonstration only.)

Before you can plot the graph, you need to exclude the placeholder data in columns C and D by following these steps:

Selecting multiple columns

1. Click column C's header, hold down the left mouse button, and drag through column D.

2. With both columns selected, choose Exclude Row/Col from Graph's Data menu.

The View Datasheet button

3. Click the View Datasheet button on Graph's Standard toolbar or choose Datasheet from Graph's View menu to remove the datasheet. The new column chart looks like this:

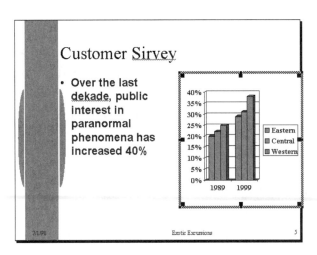

You can now move or resize the chart using the same steps you used to move and resize graphics.

Changing the Chart Type

With Graph, you can easily switch to a different chart type if you don't like the way your data is displayed. For a clearer representation, change the chart type on Slide 5 by following these steps:

The Chart Type button

1. Click the arrow to the right of the Chart Type button on Graph's Standard toolbar to display the palette of options shown at the top of the facing page.

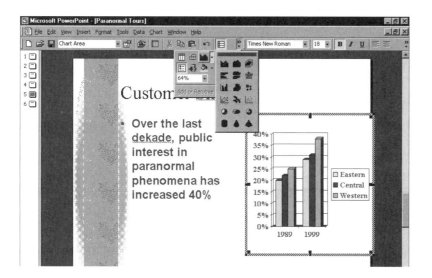

2. Select one of the palette's options and notice the effect it has on the chart. Then experiment with other chart types to get a feel for what's available.

3. When you're ready to move on, click the Line Chart option (the fourth option in the left column) to switch to a line chart. The results are shown here:

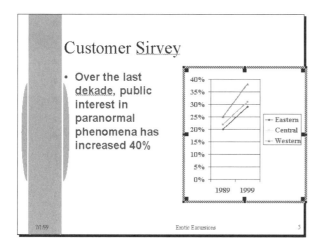

Now follow these steps to learn another way of switching chart types:

1. Choose Chart Type from Graph's Chart menu to display the Chart Type dialog box shown on the next page.

The default graph format

Initially, Graph creates a graph in its default format, which is a three-dimensional column chart. To change the default format, choose Chart Type from Graph's Chart menu and make a selection on the Standard Types or Custom Types tab of the Chart Type dialog box. Then click the Set As Default Chart button at the bottom of the dialog box. When PowerPoint displays a message box to confirm your selection, click Yes. After you click OK in the Chart Type dialog box, the new default chart type goes into effect immediately and remains in effect until you change it.

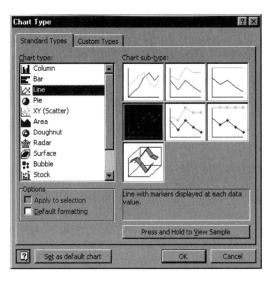

On the Standard Types tab, all the available chart types are listed on the left and the sub-types for the selected type are displayed on the right. The current type is highlighted. Clicking a sub-type displays its description in the box below. If none of the standard types fits the bill, PowerPoint provides 20 additional options on the Custom Types tab, including combination graphs (see the adjacent tip).

2. Click the Custom Types tab to display these options:

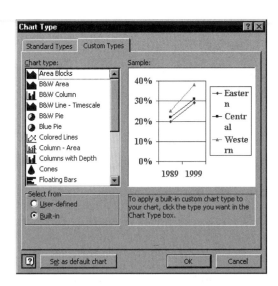

Combination graphs

If you want to create a combination graph, simply select one of the combination types on the Custom Types tab of the Chart Type dialog box. You can plot your data as one type overlaid by another type, such as a column chart overlaid by a line chart. Or if your data includes series that span widely divergent ranges of values, you can plot a data series against a y-axis scale on the left side of the graph and another data series against a y-axis scale on the right side of the graph.

3. Explore the chart types available on both the Custom Types and Standard Types tabs.

4. When you finish exploring, select Column on the Standard Types tab and select the two-dimensional clustered column sub-type. Then click OK to close the Chart Type dialog box and return to Slide 5 with the chart redrawn according to your instructions.

Customizing Graphs

Before you can make any adjustments to a graph, you must select the graph object you want to change. If Graph is still open, you can select a graph object simply by clicking it with the mouse. Colored handles surround the object to indicate that it is selected. If you are working in PowerPoint, you can quickly start Graph by double-clicking the current graph or by clicking the graph once and pressing Enter. You can then click the graph object you want to modify.

Selecting graph objects

After you select a graph object, you can choose the Selected *Object* command from Graph's Format menu to open a dialog box with options related to the selected object. You can also open the Format dialog box by clicking the Format button on Graph's Standard toolbar; by right-clicking a graph object and choosing the Format *Object* command from the shortcut menu; or by double-clicking the graph object.

The Format button

If you're a little baffled by all this, don't worry—we'll walk you through the entire process in a moment. Before we do, however, take a minute or two to study the following figure, which depicts the graph objects on a typical graph:

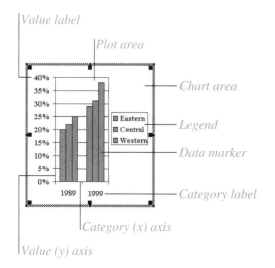

Value label

Plot area

Chart area

Legend

Data marker

Category label

Category (x) axis

Value (y) axis

The Chart Objects box

If an object is hard to select with the mouse, an easy solution is to click the arrow to the right of the Chart Objects box on Graph's Standard toolbar and select the desired object from the drop-down list.

Working with Titles

You can add a title to the graph, the category (x) axis, the value (y) axis, or all three. You can then format the title or titles using the Format dialog box. Try this:

1. With Graph open (if it isn't, double-click the column chart on Slide 5 to start the program), choose Chart Options from Graph's Chart menu. If necessary, click the Titles tab to display these options:

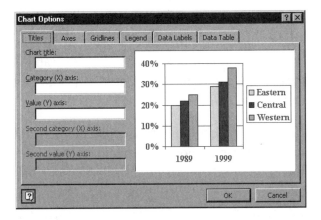

2. In the Chart Title edit box, type *U.S. Regional Interest* and check out the new title in the preview box. Then click OK.

3. With the title selected (surrounded by handles), choose Selected Chart Title from Graph's Format menu and click the Font tab to see these options:

Adding an axis title

To add a title to a graph's axis, choose the Chart Options command from Graph's Chart menu. Enter a title in the appropriate edit box on the Titles tab of the Chart Options dialog box, and click OK. You can then rotate the selected title by choosing Selected Axis Title from Graph's Format menu, clicking the Alignment tab of the Format Axis Title dialog box, and changing the Degrees setting in the Orientation section.

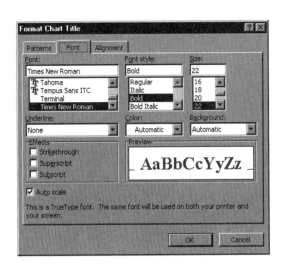

4. Change the font to Arial and the size to 18. Then click OK.

Working with Legends

By default, Graph added a legend to the column chart on Slide 5. If a graph does not have a legend, you can add one on the Legend tab of the Chart Options dialog box. To remove a legend, simply select it and press the Delete key.

Adding or deleting a legend

Because a legend is a graph object, you can format it using the same techniques described for other graph objects. You can select the legend and then choose Selected Legend from Graph's Format menu; right-click the legend and choose Format Legend from the shortcut menu; or double-click the legend. When the Format Legend dialog box appears, use the options on the Patterns, Font, and Placement tabs to change the border, background, font, location, and size of the legend.

Rather than using the Placement tab to reposition and resize the legend, you can use the mouse. Follow these steps:

1. Click the legend once to select it. (Be sure the entire legend is selected, not just one of the legend entries or keys.)

2. Point to the border surrounding the legend. (Don't point to a handle.) Hold down the left mouse button, drag upward until the legend is aligned with the graph's top gridline, and then release the mouse button.

Moving a legend

3. Click anywhere in the chart area to deselect the legend. (Be careful not to click *outside* the chart area, or you'll wind up back in PowerPoint.) The graph now looks like this:

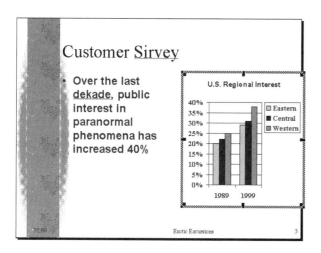

Formatting parts of a legend

You can select an entry in a legend (such as *Eastern* in the sample column chart's legend) and in the Format Legend Entry dialog box change such elements as font, font style, and size. You can also select a legend key (the small color box next to each legend entry) and change its border, color, and background using the Format Legend Key dialog box.

Types of axes ———————————————→

Working with Axes, Tick Marks, Gridlines, and Labels

The two-dimensional column graph in Paranormal Tours has two axes: the *value* or vertical y axis and the *category* or horizontal x axis. Logically, values are plotted along the value axis, and categories are plotted along the category axis. You'll find axes in all the chart types except pie and doughnut graphs. Some three-dimensional (3D) chart types, such as 3D area, 3D column, 3D line, and 3D surface graphs, have a third axis, called the *series* axis. In these graphs, the x axis remains the category axis, the y axis becomes the series axis, and the z axis becomes the value axis.

This may all sound a bit confusing, but the figures shown below should help clarify matters. The figure on the left is a two-dimensional column chart with category (x) and value (y) axes. The figure on the right is a three-dimensional column chart with category (x), series (y), and value (z) axes. Note that the three-dimensional column graph has additional graph objects called the *walls* and the *floor*, and that the value axis rises up from the floor while the category and series axes are both plotted along the floor.

Formatting with fills

To quickly add color to any graph object, select the object, click the arrow to the right of the Fill Color button on Graph's Standard toolbar, and then select the desired color. For more complex fills, select the graph object, display its Format dialog box, and click the Fill Effects button in the Area section of the Patterns tab. You can then try the gradients, textures, and patterns on their respective tabs. On the Picture tab, you can click the Select Picture button and select a picture file created in another program (such as Microsoft PhotoDraw).

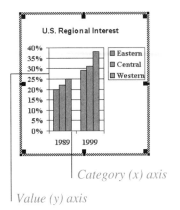

Category (x) axis

Value (y) axis

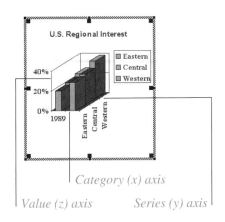

Category (x) axis

Value (z) axis   *Series (y) axis*

The small marks used to group values or categories along the axes are called *tick marks*. A graph can have major tick marks and minor tick marks, but only major tick marks appear by default. To add minor tick marks, select the axis and choose Selected Axis from Graph's Format menu. Then select one of the Minor Tick Mark Type options on the Patterns tab of the Format Axis dialog box. You can also remove or reposition the major tick marks along the selected axis.

In some cases, gridlines can make a graph more readable. The current graph has gridlines emanating from the major tick marks along the value axis, allowing you to more easily assess the values of the data markers. You can add gridlines to both major and minor tick marks by selecting from the options on the Gridlines tab of the Chart Options dialog box. After you've added gridlines, you can format them by selecting a gridline along one axis, choosing Selected Gridlines from Graph's Format menu, and then using the Patterns tab of the Format Gridlines dialog box to change the style, color, and weight of all the gridlines or the Scale tab to change the scale. (You'll change the scale in a moment.) You can remove gridlines from a graph by deselecting the appropriate options on the Gridlines tab of the Chart Options dialog box.

Removing gridlines

The column chart in Paranormal Tours sports labels along both axes. You can change the position (see the tip below), font, number format (see the tip below), and alignment of the labels. Select their corresponding axis, choose Selected Axis from Graph's Format menu, and then select options in the Format Axis dialog box.

Repositioning labels

By default, Graph places tick-mark labels next to their respective axes. To change the position of the labels, select one of the Tick Mark Labels options on the Patterns tab of the Format Axis dialog box. (If you want to open this dialog box, select an axis and then choose Selected Axis from Graph's Format menu.) Selecting the Low or High option places labels next to the minimum or maximum values. Selecting the None option removes the labels altogether.

Formatting numbers

To change the formatting of numeric tick-mark labels, display the Number tab of the Format Axis dialog box. If Linked To Source is selected, the numbers have the same formatting as the numbers in the datasheet. To apply a different format, select an option from the Category list, and then select the format you want from the list on the right. A sample of your selection appears at the top of the Number tab. To create a custom format, select the Custom option in the Category list and then enter the appropriate codes in the Type edit box.

Adding data labels

You can add labels to data markers to show the value or percent of each marker. Double-click one of the data markers to display the Format Data Series dialog box, click the Data Labels tab, select the option you want, and click OK. You can format the data labels by clicking a label to select all of them, choosing Selected Data Labels from Graph's Format menu, and then selecting options in the Format Data Labels dialog box.

The value-axis labels in the column chart on Slide 5 are a bit crowded. To reduce the crowding, you can change the scale of the axis. Follow these steps:

1. Click the arrow to the right of the Chart Objects box and select Value Axis from the drop-down list.

2. Choose Selected Axis from the Format menu and click the Scale tab of the Format Axis dialog box to display the options shown here:

Adding text boxes and arrows

To embellish your graph with text, click the Text Box button on the Drawing toolbar, position the cross-hair pointer where you want the text box to appear, hold down the left mouse button, and drag to create the box. A flashing insertion point appears inside the text box so that you can enter the text. As you type, the text automatically wraps within the invisible boundaries of the box. To reposition a text box, point to the box's border, hold down the left mouse button, and drag to a new location. To resize a text box, drag one of its handles. To delete a text box, select it and press Delete. You can connect a text box to an item in your graph by drawing an arrow. Click the Arrow button on the Drawing toolbar, position the mouse pointer at the starting point for the arrow, hold down the left mouse button, and drag to the ending point for the arrow. Like other graph objects, you can format text boxes and arrows by using the options in the Format *Object* dialog box.

3. Under Auto, the value axis is scaled from 0 to 0.4, with labels at major-unit intervals of 0.05. Double-click the Major Unit edit box (not the check box), type *0.15*, and click OK.

4. Click outside the graph to see these results in PowerPoint:

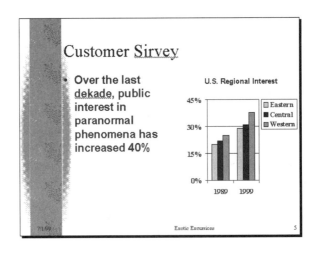

Working with Chart and Plot Areas

To give the chart area a little more distinction, you can add a border to it and change its background color. (You can use the same techniques to format the plot area.) And, rather than change the formatting of individual text elements on the graph, such as the title and tick-mark labels, you can save some time by changing the formatting of all the text at once in the Format Chart Area dialog box. Let's add a border and change the background color of the column chart on Slide 5. Follow these steps:

1. Start Graph and double-click the chart area (the blank area below the legend is a good spot). Graph displays the Format Chart Area dialog box.

2. On the Patterns tab, click the arrow to the right of the Color box in the Border section to display a color palette, and then select blue.

Adding a border

3. Next click the arrow to the right of the Weight box and select the last option (heavy).

4. Click the Shadow check box to give the border a shadow.

5. To change the color of the chart area's background, move to the Area section of the Patterns tab and select lilac (the fourth color in the first row of the bottom section of the palette).

Changing the background color

6. If you wanted to change the font and font style of all the text on the graph, you could click the Font tab and make your selections. But the font settings are fine as they are, so click OK to close the dialog box.

Changing the text font

7. Click anywhere outside the graph to return to PowerPoint, and deselect the graph. The results are shown at the top of the following page.

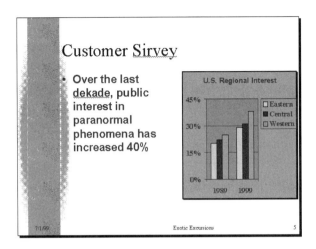

Moving and Sizing Graphs in PowerPoint

You don't have to open Microsoft Graph in order to move and resize the chart area of a graph. You can accomplish these tasks in PowerPoint, like this:

Displaying rulers

1. Choose Ruler from the View menu to turn on PowerPoint's rulers. (The rulers will serve as guides when you move and resize the graph.)

2. Click the column chart once to select it.

3. Point inside the graph's border and hold down the left mouse button. When the dashed positioning box appears, drag to the left about ½ inch, using the horizontal ruler as a guide. Then release the mouse button.

4. To increase the width of the graph, point to the right middle handle. When the pointer changes to a double-headed arrow, hold down the left mouse button and drag to the right about ¼ inch.

5. Drag the bottom border of the graph down a bit to give the category axis labels some breathing room.

6. Choose Ruler from the View menu to turn off the rulers and then deselect the graph to see the results shown at the top of the facing page.

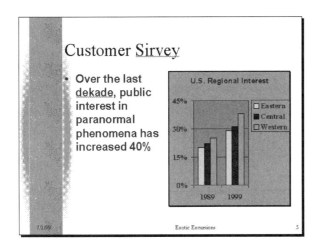

7. You're probably ready to take a break, so save the presentation and quit PowerPoint.

Traditionally, graphs and charts play a big role in presentations because they can convey large amounts of information quickly. It's worth taking the time to experiment with Graph so that you know how to take maximum advantage of this important presentation tool.

Fine-Tuning a Presentation

You create a second presentation using a design template and then switch templates. Next you format, edit, and spell-check the text of the slides, and then you adjust the order of the slides. Finally, you learn more about delivering a presentation.

These techniques will simplify the creation and delivery process, whether you are presenting a budget analysis in a corporate boardroom or an educational report in a classroom.

Slides created and concepts covered:

Customize PowerPoint's design by adding your own formatting

Create a presentation based on a design template and add the slides you need

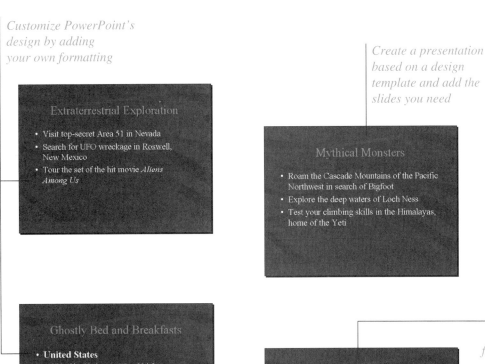

Copy and move text from slide to slide and from presentation to presentation

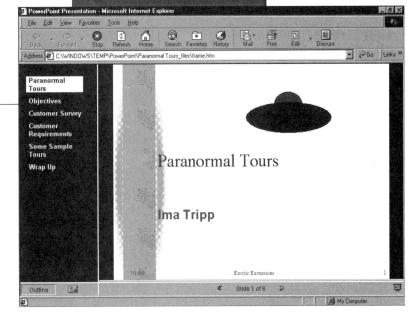

Easily convert a presentation to HTML format for Web delivery

In Chapter 1, you created a presentation using one of the AutoContent Wizard's ready-made presentation types, and then you tailored the text of its topics, bulleted items, and subordinate items to meet your needs. In this chapter, you create a new presentation based on a design template, adding slides and text as you go along. Then we show you various ways of fine-tuning your presentations by editing and formatting text and rearranging slides to strengthen your argument.

The Characteristics of a Good Presentation

Before you get going, we want to remind you of the characteristics that distinguish a good presentation from a bad one. PowerPoint, for all its fancy features, is just a tool. The overall effectiveness of your presentation depends on your thoughtful planning and attention to the smallest details. It is easy to mar a presentation produced in PowerPoint with bad characteristics, such as small fonts, extraneous details, and distracting visual embellishments. Here are some pointers for creating clear, concise slides:

The audience

- Put yourself in the shoes of your audience. You should know as much as possible about the people you're presenting to before you start creating your presentation, and then tailor its tone, words, and graphics appropriately.

The overall theme

- What points do you want your audience to remember one hour after your presentation? One week after? You can facilitate your audience's recall by coming up with an overall theme to reinforce throughout the presentation.

One main idea

- Make each slide responsible for conveying only one main idea that can be interpreted at a glance.

No extra words

- Cut the verbiage on each slide to the essentials. Never have more than six bulleted items on a slide. The more bulleted items you have, the fewer words you should use in each item.

Consistency

- Make sure your capitalization and punctuation is consistent throughout your presentation and that your slide titles are constructed in similar ways. On any one slide, don't mix complete sentences and partial sentences.

Above all, don't expect your slides to carry the entire weight of the presentation. When it comes right down to it, *you* are giving the presentation, not your visual aids. To hold the attention of your audience—large or small—you must be confident and poised, and you must express your ideas clearly and persuasively. Many day-to-day business activities—such as introducing a new product to a customer, conducting a meeting, or negotiating a contract—involve making presentations of one sort or another, with or without visual aids. The ability to speak in front of a group is a necessary skill that is worth cultivating, even if you don't anticipate ever having to address a room full of people.

Speaking skills

Using a Design Template

If you know exactly what you want to say but you need a little help coming up with a design for your presentation, you can bypass the AutoContent Wizard and start a presentation based on one of PowerPoint's design templates. A *template* is a set of ready-made formatting that defines the look of a slide. PowerPoint comes with many templates that incorporate different combinations of graphic, typographic, and special effects. Often one of these templates is just what you need to give a presentation an appropriate, professional look. And, if you later change your mind about the design you have chosen, you can easily switch to a different template with just a few mouse clicks.

Templates

Follow the steps below to create a presentation using a design template:

1. Start PowerPoint by choosing Programs and then Microsoft PowerPoint from the Start menu.

2. When the PowerPoint dialog box appears, double-click the Design Template option to open the New Presentation dialog box and display the template options as shown on the following page.

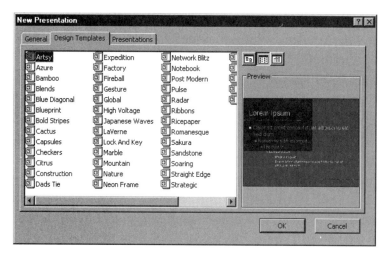

Previewing templates

3. Click each template icon in turn, and check the Preview box on the right to see which ones are installed.

4. When you're ready, double-click the Capsules icon. If this template is not installed on your computer, you may be prompted to insert the installation CD-ROM. PowerPoint then opens the New Slide dialog box, which as you see below, looks like the Slide Layout dialog box shown on page 43.

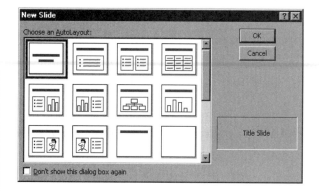

Greeked previews

The text in the Preview box of the New Presentation dialog box (*Lorem ipsum*, and so on) is traditionally used in layout work. It gives you an idea of how the publication will look when the real text is in place, without distracting you with words you can actually read. We have been unable to discover the origins of this tradition, other than that this block of random Latin words has been used for this purpose for centuries. Though the words are Latin, this type of placeholder is known as *greeked text*.

5. Scroll the Choose An Autolayout box to see all the various slide autolayouts that are available. Then scroll back to the top of the box.

6. Click the second autolayout in the top row (Bulleted List) and click OK to create a bulleted list slide.

7. Save the presentation with the name *Sample Tours*.

Slide 1's design is in place, so you can now work on the content of your presentation. Follow these steps:

1. Switch to slide view, click the title area, and enter the title *Extraterrestrial Exploration.*

2. Click the object area and type *Visit top-secret Area 51 in Nevada* as the first bulleted item.

3. Press Enter to start another bulleted item and type *Search for UFO wreckage in Roswell, New Mexico.*

4. Press Enter again and then type *Tour the set of the hit movie Aliens Among Us.* The results are shown here:

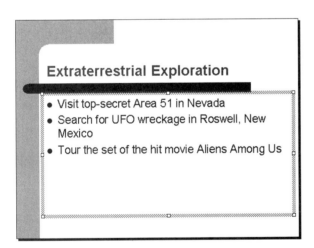

Notice that all the bulleted items begin with a verb and have the same direct, matter-of-fact tone.

Adding Slides

When you create a presentation based on a design template, PowerPoint provides only the initial slide. To add three more slides to Sample Tours, follow these steps:

1. With Slide 1 displayed on the screen, click the New Slide button on the Standard toolbar to open the New Slide dialog box.

The New Slide button

2. Be sure the Bulleted List autolayout is selected and click OK to add a second slide to your presentation.

3. Click the title area of Slide 2 and type *Mythical Monsters*.

4. In the object area, type *Roam the Cascade Mountains of the Pacific Northwest in search of Bigfoot* as the first bulleted item.

5. Press Enter, type *Explore the deep waters of Loch Ness,* press Enter again, and type *Test your climbing skills in the Himalayas, home of the Yeti.*

6. Repeat steps 1 and 2 above to add a new bulleted-list slide and then type *Ghostly Bed and Breakfasts* as the title.

7. Click the object area of Slide 3 and type the items listed here, using the Demote button on the Formatting toolbar to create the subordinate items and the Promote button to switch back to creating bulleted items:

- *United States*
  - *Visit with spirited guests at Cape Muir Inn*
  - *Participate in a séance at haunted Butterfield House*
- *Europe*
  - *Have tea with the original occupants of 17th century Langley Manor*
  - *Cavort with headless Count Meeout at Verdun Castle*

Repositioning text areas

You can use the mouse to reposition text areas on a slide. For example, to shift the title up a bit, click the title area to select it. Point to the frame surrounding the area, hold down the left mouse button, and then drag the frame upward. You can use this same technique to reposition a slide's object area. In addition, you can resize the areas by dragging the small white handles that appear when an area is selected.

8. Add a fourth bulleted-list slide and type *Bermuda Triangle Mystery Tour* as the title. Then type these bulleted items:

- *Sail with the experienced crew of the Titanic II across the Sargasso Sea*
- *Dive the waters of Bermuda and the Bahamas in search of sunken ships and planes*

9. Save the Sample Tours presentation.

Switching Templates

After creating the Extraterrestrial Exploration slide, suppose you recall seeing a design template in the New Presentation dialog box that you think would better fit the theme of this presentation. Fortunately, PowerPoint makes it easy to switch from one template to another. Here's how:

1. Move to Slide 1 of the Sample Tours presentation and then choose Apply Design Template from the Format menu to display the dialog box shown here:

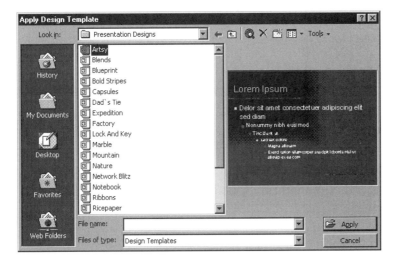

2. Scroll the list to see what's available, and then double-click the Mountain option. Slide 1 now looks like this:

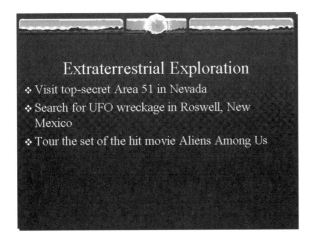

3. Scroll through the other slides in the presentation and note that the Mountain template has been applied to them all.

Although the Mountain template is a good choice for Slide 1, it's not appropriate for the other slides in the presentation. Let's check out another design template for Sample Tours:

1. Right-click the background of any displayed slide and choose Apply Design Template from the shortcut menu.

2. When the Apply Design Template dialog box appears, double-click the Ribbons option and admire the results.

Formatting Text

You have selected a design template to give your presentation a particular look but you can still use text formatting to create additional visual effects. For example, you can use the bold style and a larger font size to draw attention to major points, and the italic style and a smaller font size to de-emphasize minor points. Let's change some of the text formatting in Sample Tours using buttons on the Formatting toolbar. Follow these steps:

1. Display Slide 1 and then select only *Aliens Among Us* in the last bulleted item.

2. Slide the Formatting toolbar's move handle to the left to see all the toolbar's buttons. By looking at the Formatting toolbar, you can determine what types of formatting have been applied to the current selection. The Font box setting is

---

Don't go overboard with fonts

When selecting a font or font styles for your presentation, keep a few simple rules in mind:

• Use a maximum of two fonts per slide—one for the title and one for all the other text.

• Use only one or two font styles, such as bold or italic, per slide.

• Watch out for certain style combinations. For example, text that is both italic and outlined is very difficult to read on a monitor or overhead projector.

• Choose fonts that have "clean" shapes. For example, sans serif fonts (those without strokes at the ends of the characters) are sometimes easier to read on slides and overhead transparencies than serif fonts.

• If you're having slides or transparencies made, be sure your service bureau can output the fonts you select.

Times New Roman, and the Font Size box setting is 32. In addition, the Left Alignment and Bullets buttons appear "pressed," which indicates that the paragraph containing the current selection is a left-aligned bulleted item.

3. Click the Italic button on the Formatting toolbar to italicize the selected text.

The Italic button

4. Now move to Slide 3 and select the text of the first bulleted item, *United States*.

5. Click the arrow to the right of the Font Size box on the Formatting toolbar to display this drop-down list of sizes:

Changing the font size

6. Scroll the list and select 36. Then click the Bold button to make the text bold.

The Bold button

7. Select the text of the second bulleted item, *Europe*, and repeat steps 5 and 6 to make the text 36 points and bold.

8. Now click anywhere on the slide to deselect the text. Here are the results:

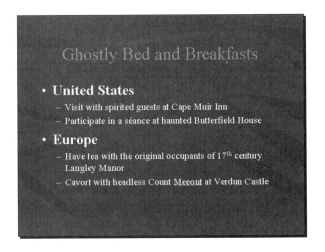

Format Painter

If you want to format a block of text with a set of formats that you have already applied to another block of text, you can copy all the formatting in a simple three-step procedure. Select the text whose formats you want to copy, click the Format Painter button on the Standard toolbar, and then select the text you want to format. Power-Point duplicates the formatting for the new selection. To format more than one block, double-click the Format Painter button, select each block in turn, and then click the button to turn it off.

The Underline button

9. Move to Slide 4, select *Titanic II* in the first bulleted item, and then click the Underline button on the Formatting toolbar.

Adding a bit of formatting here and there can certainly improve the look of a presentation. Let's make one more improvement by rebreaking a couple of lines of text on Slide 1:

1. Display Slide 1 and click an insertion point to the left of the *N* in *New* in the second bulleted item.

Rebreaking lines

2. Press Shift+Enter to break the line after *Roswell*.

3. In the last bulleted item, click an insertion point to the left of the *A* in *Among* and press Shift+Enter to break the line after *Aliens*. The text of Slide 1 now appears more balanced, as you can see here:

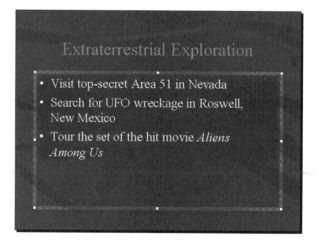

Opening an Existing Presentation

You've pretty much finished with the Sample Tours presentation, and you now want to do some more work on the Paranormal Tours presentation you created in Chapters 1 and 2. However, because these two presentations contain some of the same information, you want to keep the Sample Tours presentation close at hand. Go ahead and follow the steps on the facing page to minimize Sample Tours and then open Paranormal Tours.

Checking your style

If you are concerned about the spelling, fonts, case, or punctuation of a presentation, you can use the Office Assistant to check your work. If you have the Office Assistant turned on, PowerPoint will mark potential problems on a slide with a light bulb. To check your style, click the light bulb to display a list of options, and then click the option you want to check. To change style options, simply click Change Style Checker Options and then change options on either the Case And End Punctuation or Visual Clarity tab. (Visual Clarity checks font usage and the legibility of titles and body text.) To restore the default settings, click the Defaults button.

1. Save Sample Tours and then click the presentation window's Minimize button—the one at the right end of the menu bar. (Clicking the Minimize button on PowerPoint's title bar will minimize the entire PowerPoint window.) Sample Tours shrinks until all that is visible is a small title bar in the bottom left corner of the PowerPoint window.

Minimizing the window

2. Now click the Open button on the Standard toolbar. PowerPoint displays this dialog box:

The Open button

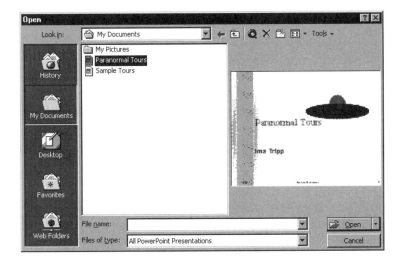

3. In the list, double-click Paranormal Tours to open it in a separate presentation window.

4. If necessary, click the window's Maximize button to expand it to fill the entire work area.

Maximizing the window

Checking Your Spelling

As you created the Paranormal Tours presentation, you deliberately included a few errors. Because PowerPoint could not find these words in its built-in or supplemental dictionary, it flagged the errors with red, wavy underlines. This feature, called *automatic spell-checking*, helps you correct errors as you work. Let's fix one of the misspelled words now:

Automatic spell-checking

1. On Slide 6, click the object area and then right-click the word *Excrusions* in the bulleted item to display the shortcut menu shown on the next page.

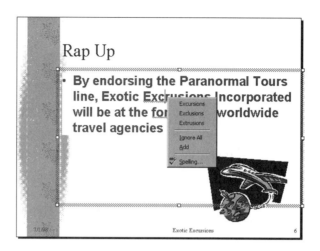

At the top of the shortcut menu, PowerPoint displays any words in its built-in and supplemental dictionaries that resemble the misspelled word. You can select one of these words, ignore the misspelling, add the word to the supplemental dictionary so that the program always recognizes this word, or move to the Spelling dialog box for more options.

2. Click *Excursions* to change the word to its correct spelling.

Here's how to check the spelling of an entire presentation:

The Spelling button

1. Move to Slide 1 and click the Spelling button on the Standard toolbar. PowerPoint switches to normal view and starts spell-checking the presentation. When it stops on *Ima*, it displays the dialog box shown on the facing page.

AutoCorrect

PowerPoint's AutoCorrect feature corrects simple typos as you enter text on a slide. For example, if you type *teh*, AutoCorrect automatically replaces it with *the*. By default, AutoCorrect also corrects two initial capital letters, such as *TRavel*, and capitalizes the names of days. To have Auto-Correct take care of your own commonly misspelled entries, choose AutoCorrect from the Tools menu. In the AutoCorrect dialog box, type the misspelling in the Replace edit box, type the correct spelling in the With edit box, and click Add. AutoCorrect adds the new entry to its list of common misspellings. (You might want to peruse this list to get a feel for the kinds of words and symbols AutoCorrect fixes by default.) You can delete entries from AutoCorrect's list by selecting the entry and clicking the Delete button. To turn the AutoCorrect feature off, select the Replace Text As You Type option in the AutoCorrect dialog box.

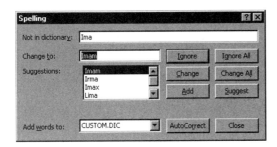

Possible substitutes for *Ima* appear in the Suggestions list, with the closest match to the unrecognized word displayed in the Change To edit box.

2. *Ima* is spelled correctly, so click Ignore to tell PowerPoint that you want to keep this name as it is.

3. Next PowerPoint stops on *paranormalism*, which is spelled correctly but is not recognized by PowerPoint. Click Add to include *paranormalism* in the supplemental dictionary, which is called Custom.dic.

Adding a word to a dictionary

4. PowerPoint stops on *Sirvey*, which is a genuine misspelling. With *Survey* in the Change To box, click Change.

5. PowerPoint stops on *dekade* and *forfront*, which are also misspelled. Click Change to substitute the correct spellings.

6. When PowerPoint reaches the end of the presentation, it closes the Spelling dialog box, and displays a message that the check is complete. Click OK to return to the presentation.

7. Unfortunately, you're not done yet. The presentation includes a word that does appear in the dictionary but is not correct in the context in which it is used. Proofread the presentation carefully to find and correct the error.

More Editing Techniques

The spell check helped clean up several errors. However, the presentation could still use a little editing. In this section, we'll show you some more ways to make editorial changes to a presentation.

Moving and Copying Text on Slides

Like most other Windows applications, PowerPoint provides two methods for moving text. The first involves cutting and pasting, which is useful for moving text from one slide to another. The second method involves dragging and dropping, which is useful for moving text to a new location on the same slide. Two similar methods are provided for copying text.

As a demonstration of these procedures, let's experiment with the text of Paranormal Tours. Follow these steps:

1. Switch to Slide view and move to Slide 3.

The Cut button

The Copy button

2. Select the text of the last bulleted item on the slide. Then click the Cut button on the Standard toolbar, or right-click the selection and choose Cut from the shortcut menu. The text is removed from the slide and stored temporarily on the Clipboard (see the tip on the facing page). If you want to copy this text instead of moving it, click the Copy button or choose the Copy command.

3. Move to Slide 2, click an insertion point after the second bulleted item, and press Enter to add a third bullet.

The Paste button

4. Click the Paste button on the Standard toolbar, or right-click the third bullet and then choose the Paste command from the shortcut menu.

5. Edit the text to read *To create tour packages that are flexible*.

Now try dragging and dropping:

1. Return to Slide 3, and in the first bulleted item, double-click *insightful* to select it.

Drag-and-drop editing

2. Point to the selection, hold down the left mouse button, and drag to the end of the first bulleted item, releasing the mouse button when the shadow insertion point is to the right of the last *e* in *enjoyable*. PowerPoint moves the selection to the end of the line, adjusting the spaces appropriately.

3. Next select the word *enjoyable* in the first bulleted item. Point to the selection, hold down the left mouse button, and drag the

shadow insertion point to the left of the *b* in *but*. After you release the mouse button, click anywhere to remove the highlight. Here are the results:

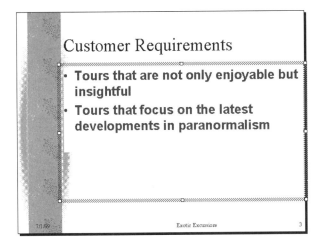

To copy text using drag-and-drop, hold down the Ctrl key while dragging the selection.

Now let's use drag-and-drop with a "twist":

1. Move to Slide 6 and select *worldwide* in the bulleted item.

2. Point to the selection, hold down the right mouse button, and drag to the end of the bulleted item. When you release the mouse button, the shortcut menu shown here appears:

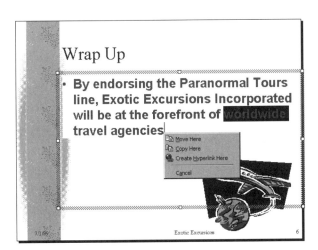

3. Choose Move Here from the menu to relocate the selection, and then save the presentation.

The Office Clipboard

In PowerPoint, you have access to two Clipboards. The Windows Clipboard stores only your most recent cut or copied item, but the Office Clipboard stores up to 12 items. So if you want to cut or copy several items from one or more presentations and paste them elsewhere, you can do so easily. After selecting one item and clicking the Cut or Copy button, cutting or copying another item displays the Clipboard toolbar, where each item is represented by the icon of the program in which it was created. (The Office Clipboard stores items from any Windows application.) Point to an icon to have ScreenTips display its contents. To paste an item, simply click an insertion point where you want it and then click the icon that represents the item you want to paste. To paste all of the items at once, click the Paste All button on the Clipboard toolbar. To clear items from the Office Clipboard, click the Clear Clipboard button. If you want to turn off the Clipboard toolbar, simply click its Close button.

Moving and Copying Text Between Presentations

We've shown you how to move and copy text in the same presentation. As you'll see in the following steps, moving and copying between presentations is equally easy:

1. Display Slide 4 and notice that the Bermuda Triangle Mystery Tour is not included in the bulleted list of sample tours.

Switching presentations

2. Choose Sample Tours from the bottom of the Window menu to activate the Sample Tours presentation.

3. Move to Slide 4 and select the slide title, *Bermuda Triangle Mystery Tour*.

4. Click the Copy button on the Standard toolbar, and then click the Paranormal Tours button on the Windows taskbar to activate that presentation.

5. With Slide 4 of Paranormal Tours displayed on your screen, click an insertion point after the last bulleted item and press Enter to create a new bulleted item.

6. Without moving the insertion point, click the Paste button on the Standard toolbar to paste the text copied from the Sample Tours presentation. As you can see, the formatting of the slide title has been replaced with the formatting of a bulleted item in this presentation's template.

Sizing the object area

7. Drag the right middle handle of the object area until the name of each tour is displayed on one line.

To move text between slides in different presentations, simply use the Cut button instead of the Copy button.

Moving and copying with the keyboard

To use the keyboard to cut text, select the text and press Ctrl+X. To then paste it, click an insertion point and press Ctrl+V. To copy text instead of moving it, follow the same procedure but use Ctrl+C instead of Ctrl+X.

Reordering Slide Text in Outline View

You can change the order of bulleted items on a slide by using cut-and-paste techniques in slide view. But reordering items is even more simple in outline view, where you can see all the topics and bulleted lists of the presentation in outline form. You can also edit slide text in outline view, but this view really shines when it's time to organize a presentation. Organizing is often a trial-and-error process. You start by evaluating the major topics, add and delete a few subtopics, and then move items around and change their levels. This task is easiest to accomplish in outline view because the Outlining toolbar puts the tools needed for organizing a presentation close at hand. Try this out now:

1. Click the Outline View button or choose Outline from the View menu.

The Outline View button

2. Right-click the toolbar row and choose Outlining from the toolbar's shortcut menu to display the Outlining toolbar.

3. Click the bullet to the left of *Extraterrestrial Exploration* on Slide 4, and then click the Move Up button on the Outlining toolbar until the selected item sits above *Ghostly Bed and Breakfasts*.

The Move Up button

4. Now click the bullet to the left of *Europe* and click the Move Down button. *Europe* and *United States* effectively switch places.

The Move Down button

5. Click the bullet to the left of *Ghostly Bed and Breakfasts*. PowerPoint selects not only the text adjacent to the bullet but also its two subordinate items.

6. Click the Move Down button twice. PowerPoint moves the main bullet and its subordinate points to the bottom of the *Some Sample Tours* list, which now looks like this:

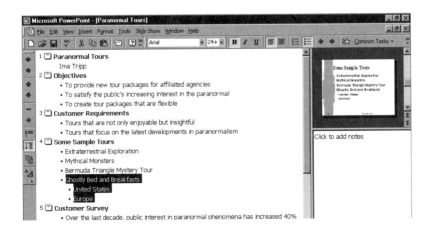

Now let's try another method you can use to rearrange bulleted items. Follow the steps below to drag an item to a new location on a slide:

Reordering by dragging

1. To begin, click the bullet to the left of the second bulleted item on Slide 2.

2. Point to the selection, hold down the left mouse button, and drag the shadow insertion point until it sits to the left of the *To* in the first bulleted item.

3. Release the mouse button. PowerPoint moves the selection to the left of the first bulleted item at the top of the list. The result is that the two bulleted items switch places.

Rearranging a Presentation

When fine-tuning a presentation, you not only need to refine the order of the text on each slide but you also need to pay attention to the order of the slides themselves. In the following section, we discuss two ways of rearranging the slides of a presentation.

Reordering Slides in Outline View

As you scroll through the presentation's outline, you might notice a slide or two that would work better in a different location. However, if the outline is too long to fit on the screen in its entirety, you may have a hard time deciding on a precise order for the slides. This "can't see the forest for the trees" situation is easily remedied by *collapsing* the outline so that only the main topics are visible. You can then move a topic up or down in the outline to change the order of the presentation's slides. Try this:

The Collapse All button

1. Click the Collapse All button on the Outlining toolbar. PowerPoint hides all the bulleted items and puts a gray line under the topics to indicate the presence of hidden information, as shown at the top of the facing page.

2. Click the slide icon for Slide 5 to select the slide topic and its hidden text, and then click the Move Up button once. *Customer Survey* is now the fourth slide in the outline.

3. Verify that the hidden text moved with the topic by clicking the Expand button on the Outlining toolbar to see this result:

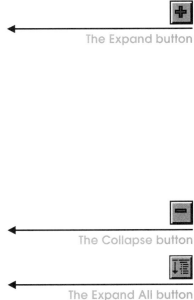

The Expand button

4. Click the Collapse button to once again hide the bulleted item.

The Collapse button

5. To redisplay the entire outline in its new order, simply click the Expand All button. Then save the presentation.

The Expand All button

Reordering Slides in Slide Sorter View

You've worked on individual slides in slide view and on the presentation outline in outline view. Now let's look at the slides from a different perspective. Slide sorter view gives you a visual overview of the presentation, where you can address issues such as slide sequencing. Here's how to rearrange slides in slide sorter view:

1. Press Ctrl+Home to move to the first slide and then click the Slide Sorter View button in the bottom left corner of the work area. When PowerPoint finishes redrawing your screen, it looks like the one shown on the next page.

The Slide Sorter View button

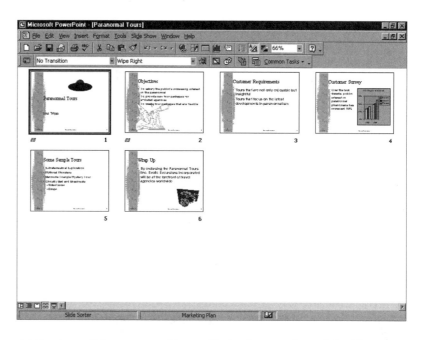

At the top of the screen, PowerPoint has replaced the Formatting toolbar with the Slide Sorter toolbar. (You might want to read the tip below and use ScreenTips to familiarize yourself with the buttons on this toolbar.) *Thumbnails*—small sketches—of the presentation's six slides are displayed with enough detail to give a good idea of how the slides look. Below Slides 1 and 2 are icons indicating that you have applied animation effects to these two slides. Because you moved to Slide 1 in the outline before clicking the Slide Sorter View button, Slide 1 is selected, as indicated by the heavy border.

Thumbnails

2. Point to Slide 4, hold down the left mouse button, drag the shadow insertion point to the left of Slide 3, and release the mouse button. Slides 3 and 4 switch places.

Changing the Thumbnail Size

When a presentation has many slides, not all of them will be visible on your screen, making it difficult to work with the entire presentation in slide sorter view. Fortunately, you can tell PowerPoint to make the slide thumbnails smaller so that you can see more slides on the screen at the same time. (The smallest size is 20% of full size.) When you work with small thumbnails, it's a good idea to also tell PowerPoint not to

The Slide Sorter toolbar

You can use the buttons and boxes on the Slide Sorter toolbar to add fancy transitions from one slide to the next. Other buttons and boxes on this toolbar provide additional ways to add animation effects to your slides.

bother displaying the slides' formatting. This saves time because PowerPoint does not have to "redraw" the slides every time you make a change to the presentation. Let's experiment:

1. Click the Show Formatting button on the Standard toolbar to toggle it off. Now the slides display only their titles in black type on a white background.

The Show Formatting button

2. Click the arrow to the right of the Zoom box on the Standard toolbar, and select 33% from the drop-down list. Your screen now looks like this:

The Zoom box

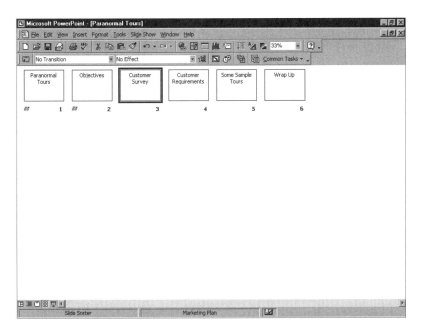

3. Click 33% in the Zoom box to highlight it, type *80*, and press Enter. PowerPoint redraws the thumbnails at 80%.

4. You're done experimenting with the thumbnail size. Restore the zoom percentage to 66%, click the Show Formatting button to redisplay the bulleted items and formatting, and then save the presentation.

5. Choose Sample Tours from the Window menu and then close it by clicking its Close button. Click Yes if asked whether you want to save your changes.

Adding Transitions

While working in slide sorter view, we'll show you how to add a type of animation, called a *transition*, to your slides. Transitions are visual and/or sound effects that you apply to a slide to help move the audience smoothly from one slide to the next, without the jerkiness associated with the replacement of one slide by another. Let's add transitions to all the slides of Paranormal Tours except the title slide:

Selecting all the slides

1. In slide sorter view, select all the slides by choosing Select All from the Edit menu. Then hold down the Ctrl key and click the title slide to deselect it. Now any commands you choose will affect all slides except the title slide.

The Slide Transition Effects box

2. Click the arrow to the right of the Slide Transition Effects box on the Slide Sorter toolbar. Select Blinds Vertical from the drop-down list and watch Slide 2 carefully as PowerPoint demonstrates the effect of the transition you have selected. Notice that PowerPoint displays a transition icon below the slides with transitions.

Testing transitions

3. Click the title slide to select it. Then switch to slide show view and click the left mouse button to run the slide show with the specified transition effect.

4. When PowerPoint switches back to slide sorter view, experiment with other transition effects. For example, try applying a different effect to each slide.

The Slide Transition button

5. Select Slides 2 and 3, and click the Slide Transition button on the Slide Sorter toolbar to display this dialog box:

6. In the Effect section, click the Slow option and then click Apply. Then select Slide 1 and rerun the slide show with the transitions at this new speed.

Changing the transition speed

7. Now apply the Wipe Left transition to all the slides except the title slide. Reset the speed to Fast, select Slide 1, and then run through the slide show to test these transition settings.

As you've probably realized, it's easy to overdo transitions. Your audience will find these special effects less distracting if you stick to one kind of transition for all your slides and if you stick with the fast speed to keep them focused on the content of your presentation rather than its mechanics.

Delivering a Presentation

When you created the Paranormal Tours presentation, the AutoContent Wizard gave you the following output options: On-Screen Presentation, Black And White Overheads, Color Overheads, and 35mm Slides. Depending on such factors as the presentation type and the size of your audience, you might need to use any of these options. We talked briefly about on-screen presentations, or electronic slide shows, in Chapter 1. Here, we'll look at some more delivery options.

Printing Transparencies

In spite of all the advances in presentation technology, black-and-white or color overhead transparencies are still the medium of choice for some people. Although the price of display equipment is falling, these people don't want or need to purchase special equipment for the rare occasions when they are called upon to make a presentation. If making presentations is part of your job or if your future career hinges on the impact of a particular presentation, you will probably discount transparencies in favor of an electronic slide show. But be warned: no amount of high-tech gadgetry can make up for a mediocre delivery style. When all is said and done, what you say—not what you show your audience—will win them over.

In this section, we give instructions for printing black-and-white transparencies, but the steps for printing color transparencies are about the same. If you have a color printer at your

Grayscale preview

If you want to see how a presentation looks in black and white, click the Grayscale Preview button on the Standard toolbar. A color slide miniature shows the underlying color design. (If this slide miniature does not appear automatically, choose Slide Miniature from the View menu to turn it on.) Click the Grayscale Preview button again to return to color view and to close the color slide miniature.

disposal, feel free to print color transparencies instead. Let's get started:

1. Turn on your printer and load the paper tray with at least six sheets of acetate. (Acetate is usually available at most office supply stores.)

2. To avoid confusion about what you are printing, switch to slide view and display Slide 1 of Paranormal Tours.

Setting up the pages →

3. Next choose Page Setup from the File menu to display this dialog box:

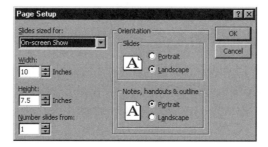

4. Click the arrow to the right of the Slides Sized For box, select Overhead from the drop-down list, and then click OK. Now the slide images will fill the acetate pages.

5. Choose Print from the File menu to display a Print dialog box like this one:

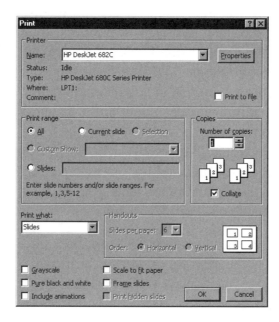

Speaker's notes

During a presentation, it can be helpful to have notes handy to keep things flowing smoothly. You can create speaker's notes while you develop the presentation. With your slide displayed in normal or outline view, click an insertion point in the Click To Add Notes section and enter text about that slide. You can also create notes for your audience to see; this can be particularly useful when your presentation is delivered via the Web. After you type in your notes as usual, simply save your presentation as a Web page and your notes automatically appear with each slide. To print speaker's notes, choose Print from the File menu, select Notes Pages in the Print What edit box, and click OK.

The Print button

(To print the entire presentation with the default settings, you can simply click the Print button on the Standard toolbar. To print only the active slide or only specific slides, or to change any of the options at the bottom of the Print dialog box, you must choose the Print command.)

6. Select Pure Black And White at the bottom of the dialog box and click OK. (If your printer can handle shades of gray, select Grayscale instead.) PowerPoint prints a transparency for each of the slides in the presentation.

Now all you need is an overhead projector and an audience, and you're ready to give your first presentation.

Printing Handouts

If you want to provide handouts so that your audience has a paper copy of the material you are presenting, you can print as many as six slides per sheet of paper. Let's print handouts for the Paranormal Tours presentation:

1. With Slide 1 displayed on your screen, choose Print from the File menu.

2. When the Print dialog box appears, click the arrow to the right of the Print What box and select Handouts.

3. In the Handout section, click the arrow to the right of the Slides Per Page box and select 2.

4. Click OK to print three handout pages.

Preparing a File for Slides

The simplest way to output a presentation as a set of 35mm slides is to entrust the imaging procedure to Genigraphics, a service bureau located in Memphis, TN. You prepare the presentation file for outputting as slides by "printing" the file using the Genigraphics software that comes with PowerPoint. A communications program called GraphicsLink is also included so that if you have a modem, you can simply send the presentation file to Genigraphics electronically. Otherwise, you can send the file on disk. You can check with local service bureaus to see whether they can also output a PowerPoint

Creating handouts in Word

If you have Microsoft Word installed on your computer, you have more options for producing notes and handouts for your presentations. Switch to black and white view by clicking the Grayscale Preview button on the Standard toolbar. Then choose Send To and Microsoft Word from the File menu. When PowerPoint displays the Write-Up dialog box, select from several layout options or the Outline Only option. Then select either Paste or Paste Link at the bottom of the dialog box and click OK. Word opens and creates the notes or handouts in the layout you selected. If you selected Paste, then the slides are embedded as-is in the Word document. If you selected Paste Link, the document's slide images are linked to the presentation's slides and will be updated to reflect any changes you make to the presentation.

presentation as 35mm slides. (See PowerPoint's Help feature for more information.) As well as 35mm slides, service bureaus can output other presentation media, such as color transparencies, copies or photographic prints, and posters. They can often also help with other electronic multimedia services.

Delivering a Presentation over the Internet or an Intranet

You can save your PowerPoint presentation as an HTML (HyperText Markup Language) document so that it can be viewed in a Web browser. Follow these steps to view and then convert Paranormal Tours:

1. Choose Page Setup from the File Menu, change the Slides Sized For setting to On-screen Show, and click OK.

2. With Paranormal Tours open, choose Web Page Preview from the File menu. Internet Explorer starts, converts the presentation file temporarily to HTML, and displays it as shown here:

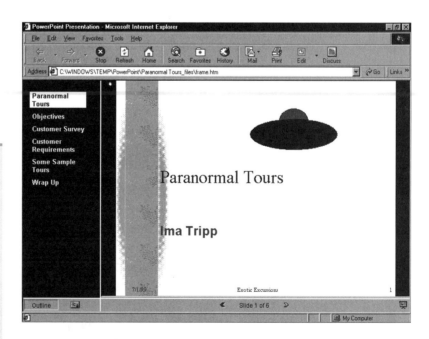

Viewing a Web presentation

You do not need to have Power-Point on your computer to view a presentation that has been saved as an HTML file; all you need is a Web browser such as Internet Explorer. You can view the presentation at any time by entering the file's path in the Address bar. You can also choose Open from the browser's File menu, click Browse, navigate to the folder where your file is saved, and then open the file.

3. Click the text hyperlinks in the left pane to jump from slide to slide.

4. Click Internet Explorer's Close button to close it and return to PowerPoint.

Everything looks good, so let's go ahead and convert the presentation to HTML:

1. Choose Save As Web Page from the File menu to display this dialog box:

Converting a presentation to HTML

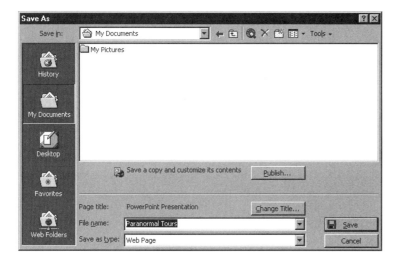

2. Click the Publish button to display this dialog box:

3. Deselect the Display Speaker Notes check box and leave the settings in the Browser Support section as they are.

4. Click the Change button to the right of Page Title in the Publish A Copy As section. Type *Paranormal Tours Web Presentation* as the new title and click OK.

Saving on a Web server

To save a file on a Web server, click the Web Folders icon in the Save As dialog box to display the locations that are available to you. Select the Web location you want to use and then click Save. To set up the Web locations so that they can be accessed from the Web Folders icon, open Windows Explorer and click Web Folders. Next double-click Add Web Folder to work through a series of dialog boxes that help you specify the URL of the Web location you want to add.

5. Check that the path in the File Name edit box reflects the location where you want to store the HTML file. Then click the Open Published Web Page In Browser check box to select it and click Publish. PowerPoint embeds the codes necessary to view the presentation with a Web browser, saves the file as Paranormal Tours.htm in the location you specified, and hands control over to Internet Explorer. You then see Slide 1 of the presentation, looking just like the screen shown earlier on page 84.

6. Look through your presentation slides either by clicking the slide title on the left side of the window or by clicking the arrows below the slide.

7. Click Internet Explorer's Close button and then PowerPoint's Close button, clicking Yes to save any changes.

If your organization uses an intranet or a Web site to distribute information, you might want to take some time to explore PowerPoint's Web publishing capabilities more thoroughly. Because you don't have to worry about what kind of computer or operating system people will use to view your presentation or even whether they have PowerPoint installed, you may well find that HTML presentations are the ideal way of distributing information when it's hard to get everyone together in the same room at the same time.

Congratulations! You have now created a couple of PowerPoint presentations and the skills you've learned should allow you to create others on your own.

Viewing HTML Coding

To get an idea of the behind-the-scenes work that PowerPoint does to make it easy for you to deliver your presentation over the Internet, you can view the underlying HTML coding. To see the codes, first choose Source from Internet Explorer's View menu. Internet Explorer then opens the file in a separate Notepad window, displaying a dizzying array of characters that actually translate into the HTML version of your presentation!

BUILDING PROFICIENCY

In Part Two, we build on the techniques covered in Part One to create a more sophisticated presentation. After completing these chapters, you'll be able to create presentations that dazzle your audience. In Chapter 4, you learn more ways to convey information visually. You create an organization chart and a table and then you use WordArt to add visual appeal to your presentation's title slide. In Chapter 5, you design a custom template using PowerPoint's slide master, and then you apply the template to an existing presentation. In Chapter 6, we wrap up the book with a more in-depth discussion of running electronic slide shows.

4

More Visual Effects

You explore another way to convey information visually by creating an organization chart. Then you learn how to create and edit tables. Finally, you use WordArt and the PowerPoint drawing tools to add other visual elements to your presentations.

The skills you gain in this chapter can be applied to any presentation that needs to convey information clearly and efficiently, such as company expense reports, market trends, or scientific data.

Slides created and concepts covered:

Use WordArt to create fancy, three-dimensional titles

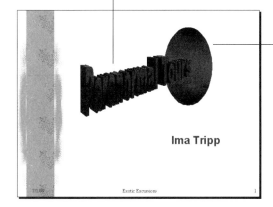

Ima Tripp

7/1/99   Exotic Excursions   1

Draw simple objects using the tools on PowerPoint's Drawing toolbar

Affiliated Agencies

Exotic Excursions Incorporated
Menlo Park, CA

Exotic Excursions Northwest
Olympia, WA
Regional Office

Pioneer Travel
Portland, OR

Globetrotter Travel
Seattle, WA

Oregon City, OR | Astoria, OR | Kirkland, WA | Poulsbo, WA

Bellevue, WA

7/1/99   Exotic Excursions   6

Make relationships or steps in a process clear with organization charts

Typical Tour Package Prices

Paranormal Tours			
Tour	Airfare	Hotel	Transport
ET Exploration	$200	$475	$120
Ghostly B&Bs, US	$480	$695	$230
Ghostly B&Bs, Europe	$798	$1,350	$360
Bermuda Triangle	$566	$1,029	$345

7/1/99   Exotic Excursions   7

Create tables to allow easy comparisons of data

I n Part One, you learned how to use PowerPoint's design templates, clip art, and graphs to provide graphic enhancements for your presentations. This chapter focuses on more methods you can use to convey information visually or graphically to enrich your slides. With PowerPoint's resources, you can add an organization chart to illustrate a company's hierarchy, or create a table to categorize and compare information. You can also add extra flourishes with fancy text created with the WordArt program. If PowerPoint's Clip Gallery doesn't provide the exact graphic you need, you can use the drawing tools to create the right image.

Adding Organization Charts

Adding graphs to your slides isn't the only way to include visual information in your presentations. In the illustrations at the beginning of the chapter, you can see that an organization chart, henceforth known as an *org chart*, has been added to Slide 5 of the Paranormal Tours presentation. Org charts are useful for illustrating hierarchies such as the executive branch of a corporation, where the CEO occupies the top position and a president, vice presidents, and so on, occupy subordinate positions. However, the basic org chart elements can also be used to develop flowcharts that illustrate the steps involved in any process.

Here's how to create an org chart slide:

1. Start PowerPoint and open Paranormal Tours. If necessary turn off the Outlining toolbar by right-clicking it and choosing Outlining from the shortcut menu.

2. Move to Slide 5, click the New Slide button on the Standard toolbar, and double-click the Organization Chart autolayout (the third autolayout in the second row) in the New Slide dialog box.

3. Click the title area and type *Affiliated Agencies*.

Microsoft Organization Chart

4. Double-click the placeholder to start the Microsoft Organization Chart program. (If necessary, click Yes and insert the installion CD-ROM to install the program.) Your screen should now look like the one on the facing page.

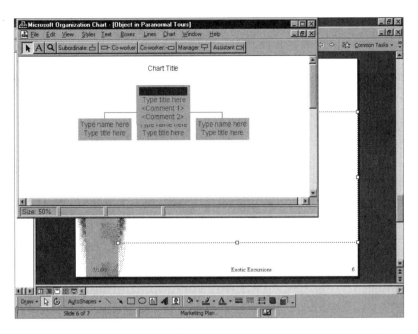

As you can see, the Org Chart window has its own menu bar, toolbar, and status bar. You use commands and buttons in this window to create an org chart and then you add it to the active slide.

5. Click the Maximize button at the right end of the Org Chart window's title bar to maximize the window.

6. Because you already gave the slide a title, select the text of the Chart Title placeholder and press Delete.

Now you're ready to fill in the org chart's boxes:

1. Click the top box to select it, then type *Exotic Excursions Northwest* as the name, and press Enter.

2. Type *Olympia, WA* as the title and press Enter.

3. For the first comment, type *Regional Office* and then click the left subordinate box to select it.

4. Type *Globetrotter Travel*, press Enter, and type *Seattle, WA*.

5. Click the center subordinate box, type *Pioneer Travel*, press Enter, type *Portland, OR*, and click outside the box. The results are shown on the next page.

Another way to add an org chart

You can change an existing slide's autolayout in order to add an org chart to the slide. Or you can simply add an org chart object to the current autolayout. Display the slide in slide view and choose Object from the Insert menu. When the Insert Object dialog box appears, check that the Create New option is selected, and then simply double-click the MS Organization Chart 2.0 option in the Object Type list. When the Org Chart program opens, complete the org chart as we describe in this chapter.

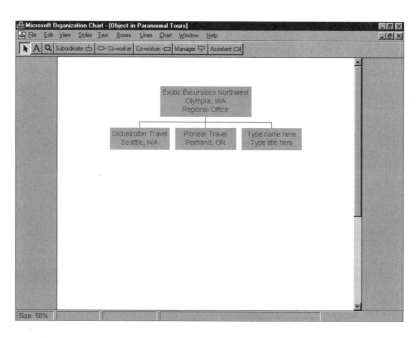

6. Don't worry about the extra placeholder box on the right. We'll deal with that in a moment. Choose the Update Paranormal Tours command from Org Chart's File menu to update the underlying slide.

Updating a presentation

To actually save the org chart as part of the presentation, you must first return to PowerPoint by clicking the Org Chart's Close button, and then choose Save from PowerPoint's File menu. To reopen the Org Chart window, you can simply double-click the org chart in PowerPoint. (To save the org chart as a separate file, use the Save Copy As command on Org Chart's File menu.)

Saving an org chart

Org chart size

Bear in mind the size of your slide when you create an org chart. If the org chart is too small, viewers may not be able to read the contents of the boxes. If the org chart consists of many boxes, consider breaking it into logical sections and placing them on separate slides so that viewers aren't overwhelmed with information.

Changing org chart defaults

Use the Options command on Org Chart's Edit menu to change the default settings for org charts. The 4-box template option (the default setting) displays the org chart template with four boxes every time you open a new org chart; the 1-box template option displays the org chart template with one box. The topmost box option displays the org chart template with one box and the formatting of the org chart that was active when you selected the option. If you want Org Chart to use the same magnification every time you open a new org chart, select the Remember The Current Magnification check box. (See page 96 for more about magnification.)

Adding and Removing Boxes

You aren't limited to the four boxes the Org Chart program has provided. You can add and remove boxes with just a few mouse clicks. Follow these steps:

The Manager button

1. To add a box to the top of the org chart, click the Manager button on the Org Chart toolbar. Then move the mouse pointer (which is now shaped like a manager box) to the top box and click once.

2. Now click the new box, type *Exotic Excursions Incorporated*, press Enter, and type *Menlo Park, CA*.

The Assistant button

3. Next click the Assistant button on the Org Chart toolbar and click the Exotic Excursions Northwest box to add an assistant box to the org chart.

4. Click the new box and type *Kirkland, WA*.

5. Add two subordinate boxes to Globetrotter Travel by clicking the Subordinate button on the Org Chart toolbar twice. (The status bar displays *Create: 2*.) Move the mouse pointer to the Globetrotter Travel box and click once. Org Chart draws two subordinate boxes below the Globetrotter Travel box.

The Subordinate button

6. In the new subordinate boxes, type *Poulsbo, WA* and then *Bellevue, WA*.

7. Repeat step 5 to add two subordinate boxes to Pioneer Travel.

Drawing lines and boxes

If the built-in box arrangements don't quite satisfy your requirements, choose Show Draw Tools from Org Chart's View menu to display four drawing tools at the right end of the Org Chart toolbar. Use the first two tools to draw perpendicular or diagonal lines, the third tool to draw connecting lines, and the fourth tool to draw boxes. To use a drawing tool, click it, position the pointer at the starting point, hold down the left mouse button, and drag to the ending point. (When you use the Auxiliary Line tool, you must drag from the edge of one existing box to the edge of another existing box.) You can resize a line or box by selecting it and dragging its handles. You can reposition a line or box by placing the pointer on the line or box border, holding down the left mouse button, and dragging to a new location in the org chart. Lines and boxes created with the drawing tools are part of the org chart's background, and they remain stationary when you move or resize the org chart itself. You should therefore finalize the org chart before you draw any lines or boxes.

8. Type *Oregon City, OR* and *Astoria, OR* in the new boxes. (Use the scroll bars to scroll the boxes into view, if necessary.)

Removing boxes

9. Remove the extraneous box to the right of the Pioneer Travel box by selecting it and then pressing the Delete key. Your org chart now looks like this:

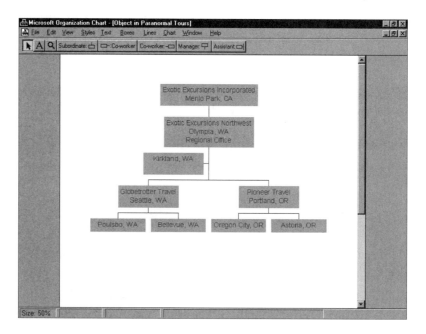

Rearranging Boxes

If you're not happy with the arrangement of boxes in an org chart, you can use the mouse to rearrange them in a variety of ways. Let's rearrange some of the boxes now:

1. Point to the Pioneer Travel box, hold down the left mouse button, and then drag the box's frame over the Globetrotter Travel box.

2. When the pointer changes to a left-pointing arrow, release the mouse button. The Globetrotter Travel and Pioneer Travel boxes switch places. (Notice that the subordinate boxes below Pioneer Travel have moved as well.)

Pointer shapes

As you've seen, the shape of the mouse pointer indicates the new position. A left-pointing arrow indicates that the box will appear to the left of the existing box, a right-pointing arrow indicates that the box will appear to the box's right, and a subordinate box indicates that the box will appear below the existing one. Try the following:

1. Drag the Kirkland, WA box's frame over the Globetrotter Travel box. Move slowly downward until the pointer changes to a subordinate box and then release the mouse button.

2. Click outside the Kirkland, WA box to deselect it. Then drag the box to the left of the Poulsbo, WA box. Here are the results after you deselect the box:

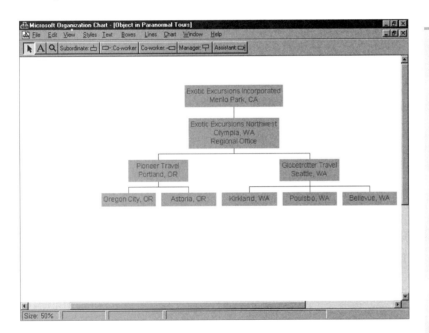

Switching Styles

Before we get into a discussion about styles, you need to become familiar with some terminology. In org chart jargon, a *group* refers to the subordinates under a manager and a *branch* refers to a manager plus all subordinates. By default, groups are placed side by side in boxes, as in the sample org chart; however, the Org Chart program offers several style alternatives for both groups and branches.

Experiment with some of the other org chart styles by following these steps:

1. First select the Kirkland, WA box and then press Ctrl+G. Notice that all three of the Globetrotter Travel subordinate boxes are now selected.

Selecting in org charts

To change the style of a group or branch, you must first select it. To select a group, you can select one member of the group and then press Ctrl+G. You can also choose Select and then Group from Org Chart's Edit menu; or you can use the selection tool on the Org Chart toolbar to draw a selection box around the group. Similarly, to select a branch, you can select one member of the branch and then press Ctrl+B. You can also choose Select and then Branch from Org Chart's Edit menu; or you can use the selection tool to draw a selection box around the branch. In addition to the Select commands on Org Chart's Edit menu, you can use the Select Levels command to select all the boxes at a specified level in your org chart. When you choose this command from the Edit menu, Org Chart displays the Select Levels dialog box, in which you enter the relevant org chart levels. For example, if your org chart has four levels and you want to select only the first three, type *1* in the first edit box, type *3* in the second edit box, and then click OK.

2. From Org Chart's Styles menu, choose the second style in the first row. The org chart now looks like this:

Magnifying an org chart

You can use the commands on Org Chart's View menu to adjust the magnification of an org chart. The following are the available commands:

- Size To Window displays the entire org chart, fitted to fill the Org Chart window.

- 50% Of Actual, or half the size of a slide, offers a balance of overview and text legibility.

- Actual Size displays the org chart at 50% larger than its printed size, giving the visual effect of a live slide show.

- 200% Of Actual, or double the size of a slide, is useful for examining your work at the greatest level of detail.

You can also use the Zoom button on the Org Chart toolbar (the button with the magnifier icon) to enlarge areas of the org chart. To return to the previous magnification, click the Zoom button (which now displays an org chart icon) again to toggle it off and then click anywhere in the org chart itself.

3. The pointer can also be used as a *selection tool* to choose more than one box. To see how, point above and to the left of the Oregon City, OR box, hold down the left mouse button, and drag a selection box around the two subordinates of Pioneer Travel. (To select boxes using this method, the selection box must completely enclose them.)

4. If two or more members of an organization share the same manager as well as the same responsibilities, they can be designated as either co-managers or co-workers. To designate the selected boxes as co-managers now, choose the Co-Manager style from Org Chart's Styles menu by clicking its icon.

Now let's condense the org chart by changing the style of its main branch:

1. With any box selected, choose Select and then All from Org Chart's Edit menu.

2. From Org Chart's Styles menu, choose the third style in the first row. Click anywhere outside the org chart to deselect the boxes and see the results shown on the facing page.

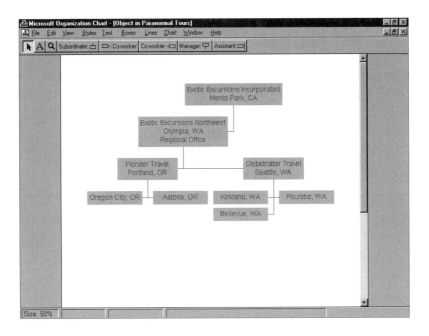

Formatting an Org Chart

Using the commands on Org Chart's Text, Boxes, and Lines menus, you can format the text, boxes, and lines in an org chart. In the following sections, you will spruce up each of these components by experimenting with various formatting options.

Formatting Org Chart Text

Org Chart's Text menu provides commands for changing the font, color, and alignment of an org chart's text. The alignment commands—Left, Right, and Center (the default)—are self-explanatory; but let's see how to change the text's font style and size so that it really stands out:

1. Select the entire org chart by pressing Ctrl+A.

2. Choose Font from Org Chart's Text menu. When the Font dialog box appears, select Bold in the Font Style list, select 18 in the Size list, and click OK.

Changing the font

Formatting Org Chart Boxes

You may want to change the appearance of the org chart's boxes so that they stand out more. Follow the steps on the next page to give them a different look.

Changing the border style 1. With all the boxes still selected, choose Border Style from Org Chart's Boxes menu to display this list of options:

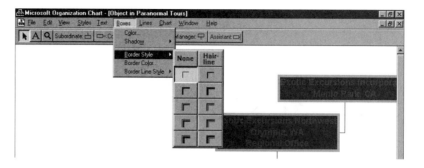

2. Select the fourth border option in the second column.

Changing the border color 3. Choose Border Color from the Boxes menu; select black, and click OK.

4. Choose Shadow from Org Chart's Boxes menu to display this list of options:

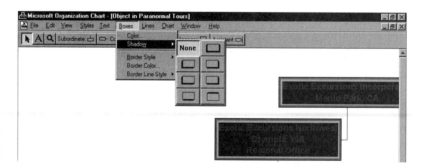

5. Select the second shadow option in the second column.

Formatting Org Chart Lines

Three commands on Org Chart's Lines menu change the thickness, style, and color of the connecting lines in an org chart. Try this:

1. Choose Select and then Connecting Lines from Org Chart's Edit menu.

2. Choose Thickness from Org Chart's Lines menu and select the third line option to increase the thickness of the lines.

Selecting lines

Before you can change lines in an org chart, you must select them. To select a single connecting line, simply click it with the mouse. To select multiple lines, hold down the Shift key and click each line, or choose Select and then Connecting Lines from Org Chart's Edit menu. You know a line is selected when it appears dotted. (If you happen to select org chart boxes as well as lines when you use the mouse, any changes you make using the commands on the Lines menu also affect the box's borders.)

3. With all the lines still selected, choose Style from Org Chart's Lines menu and select the last (dashed) line option.

4. Click anywhere outside the org chart to deselect the connecting lines, and scroll the window to see these results:

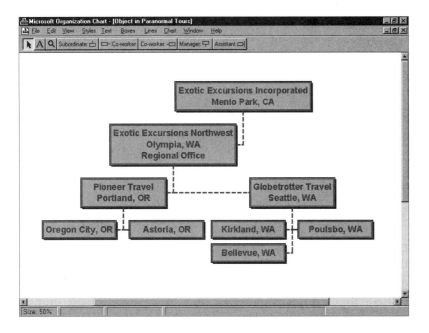

Returning to PowerPoint

After an org chart is complete, quitting Org Chart and returning to PowerPoint automatically adds the org chart to the current slide. Once the org chart is in place, you can use the mouse to reposition or resize it. (You can return to the Org Chart program at any time by double-clicking the org chart on the slide.) Let's return to PowerPoint now:

1. Choose Update Paranormal Tours from Org Chart's File menu. (If you don't choose this command first, you will be prompted to update the org chart before proceeding.)

2. Choose the Exit And Return To Paranormal Tours command from Org Chart's File menu.

Once you're back in PowerPoint, you can see that the org chart should be enlarged. Follow these steps:

1. Be sure the org chart is selected (surrounded by handles). If it isn't, click the object area once to select it.

Sizing an org chart

2. Drag the corner handles to enlarge the height and width proportionally until the org chart fills the slide, like this:

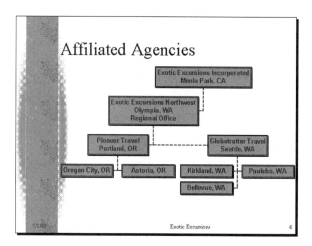

Adding Tables

Adding tables to PowerPoint slides is a snap. In the following sections, we'll show you how to add a table to a slide, enter data, modify the table's structure, and format the table. Follow these steps to get started:

Creating a table slide

1. With Slide 6 of the Paranormal Tours presentation displayed in slide view, click the New Slide button on the Standard toolbar. Then double-click the Table autolayout (the fourth autolayout in the first row).

2. Type *Typical Tour Package Prices* as the slide's title.

3. Double-click the table placeholder in the slide's object area to display this dialog box:

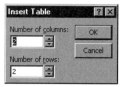

Specifying the number of columns and rows

4. Type *4* in the Number Of Columns edit box. Double-click the Number Of Rows edit box, type *5*, and then click OK. The

Tables And Borders toolbar appears and an empty table with the number of columns and rows you specified fills the object area of the slide. Your screen looks like this:

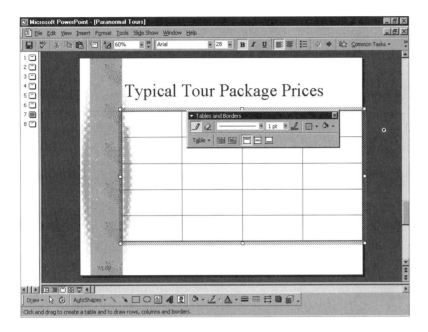

Like the datasheet in Graph (see page 44), the table is divided into units called *cells*. The borders that demarcate the cells can be turned on and off by selecting the table, clicking the arrow to the right of the Borders button on the Tables And Borders toolbar, and clicking the No Border button on the drop-down palette.

The Borders button

5. If the Tables And Borders toolbar is "floating," dock it by double-clicking its title bar.

6. If rulers appear across the top and down the left side of the table, choose Ruler from the View menu to turn them off. (You don't need the rulers right now.)

Entering Data

You enter data in a table the same way you enter it elsewhere in PowerPoint—simply by typing it. You can move the insertion point to a cell by clicking the cell with the mouse, or by using the keys and key combinations listed in the table at the top of the following page.

Another way to add a table

You can change the autolayout of an existing slide to add a table to a slide. Or you can simply add a table object to the current autolayout. Display the slide in slide view and choose Table from the Insert menu. Then go ahead and complete the Insert Table dialog box as shown on the facing page.

Moving around in a table

To move the insertion point...	Use this key(s)
Up or down one line or cell	Up or Down Arrow
Left or right one character or cell	Left or Right Arrow
To next or previous cell	Tab or Shift+Tab

If you make a mistake, press the Backspace or Delete key; to start a new paragraph within a cell, press the Enter key.

Try the following:

1. With the insertion point in the first cell of the table, type *Tour* and press Tab. Type *Airfare*, press Tab, and type *Transport*.

2. In the second cell of the first column, type *ET Exploration*, press Tab, type *$200*, press Tab again, and type *$120*.

3. Using the navigation techniques listed above, complete the table in Paranormal Tours with this information:

Ghostly B&Bs, US	*$480*	*$230*
Ghostly B&Bs, Europe	*$798*	*$360*
Bermuda Triangle	*$566*	*$345*

Your table looks something like the one shown below. (Don't worry about bad word breaks for now.)

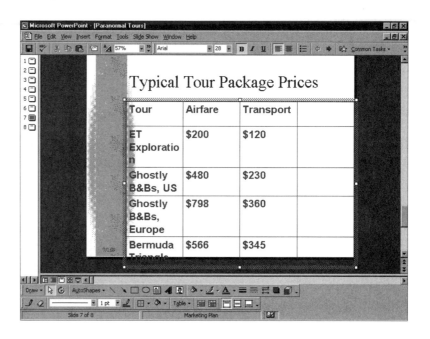

4. Point to the table's border and drag the table upwards and to the left so that you can see it all.

5. Now save the table by clicking the Save button on the Standard toolbar.

Inserting and Deleting Columns and Rows

If you need to add or remove columns or rows from your tables, the steps are simple. Let's insert a new column to the left of the Transport column in the sample table:

1. With the table active (surrounded by a shaded border and handles), click anywhere in the Transport column. Then click the Table button on the Tables And Borders toolbar and choose Select Column from the expanded menu.

2. Click the Table button again and choose Insert Columns To The Left from the button's menu. PowerPoint inserts a column to the left of the Transport column.

3. In the first cell of the new column, type *Hotel* as the column heading. Then fill in the remaining cells of the column with the information listed here:

$475
$695
$1,350
$1,029

Now insert a new row at the top of the table by following the steps on the next page.

More about selecting, inserting, and deleting

Before you can insert or delete a column or row, you must indicate where you want the insertion or deletion to take place. To select a column, either drag through the cells of the column or click any cell in the column and choose Select Column from the Table menu. You can also point to the top of the column, and when the mouse pointer changes to a down arrow, click the left mouse button. To select a row, drag through the cells of the row or click any cell in the row and choose Select Row from the Table menu. To select multiple columns or rows, drag through them. If you select multiple columns or rows before choosing the Insert or Delete command, that many columns or rows are inserted or deleted.

1. Click any cell in the first row, click the Table button, and choose Select Row from the button's menu.

2. Click the Table button again and choose Insert Rows Above from the button's menu.

3. In the first cell of the new row, type *Paranormal Tours*.

Deleting rows and columns is simple. Follow these steps:

Deleting rows and columns

1. Select the last column in the table.

2. Click the Table button and choose Delete Columns to remove the column.

Adjusting Column Width and Row Height

The fastest way to adjust column widths or row heights in a table is to move the gridlines between the columns or rows, or to move the column or row markers on the rulers. For example, to decrease the width of a column, you can drag the column's right gridline to the left. Or, to increase the height of a row, you can drag the marker that aligns with the bottom of the row downward on the vertical ruler. Follow these steps to adjust the widths of some of the columns in the sample table:

Displaying rulers

1. Choose Ruler from the View menu to turn on the horizontal and vertical rulers. You can use the rulers along the top and left sides of the screen to help set the width of columns. You can also set tabs using the horizontal ruler. A tab alignment button, currently displaying the symbol for left-aligned tabs, sits at the intersection of the rulers. You can change the tab-alignment setting simply by clicking this button. After clicking the button, you click the ruler to set a tab.

2. Choose Ruler from the View menu again to turn off both of the rulers.

3. Click an insertion point in the Tour column and point anywhere along the column's right gridline. When the pointer changes to a double bar with arrows, hold down the left mouse button and drag until ET Exploration fits on one line.

Moving and copying in tables

The fastest way to move the entries in a column, row, or cell in a table is to select them and drag them to their new location. Hold down the Ctrl key as you drag to copy, rather than move, the entries. (To move or copy multiple columns, rows, or cells, select them all before you drag.) You can also use the Cut, Copy, and Paste commands from the Edit and shortcut menus.

4. Repeat step 2, moving the right gridlines of the Airfare column, the Hotel column, and the Transport column so that each column is wide enough to hold all its contents. Here are the results:

Typical Tour Package Prices			
Paranormal Tours			
Tour	Airfare	Hotel	Transport
ET Exploration	$200	$475	$120
Ghostly B&Bs, US	$480	$695	$230
Ghostly B&Bs, Europe	$798	$1,350	$360
Bermuda Triangle	$566	$1,029	$345

Merging and Splitting Cells

To include headings that span more than one column, you can convert two or more cells to one large cell. Create a heading for the sample table by merging the cells in the first row:

1. Select any cell in the first row of the table, click the Table button, and choose Select Row from the button's menu.

2. Click the Merge Cells button on the Tables And Borders toolbar. The result is shown here:

The Merge Cells button

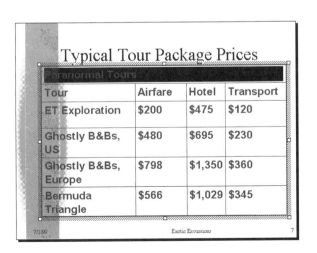

Typical Tour Package Prices			
Paranormal Tours			
Tour	Airfare	Hotel	Transport
ET Exploration	$200	$475	$120
Ghostly B&Bs, US	$480	$695	$230
Ghostly B&Bs, Europe	$798	$1,350	$360
Bermuda Triangle	$566	$1,029	$345

Moving and sizing tables

You can change the location of a table on a slide by selecting it and then using the arrow keys to move it up, down, left, or right to the desired location. To resize a table, drag its handles. If you drag one of the corner handles, you can change the height and width of the table proportionally.

If you click the Merge Cells button by mistake, you can choose Undo Merge Cells from the Edit menu to return the merged cells to their original state. If you decide later that you don't want the cells to be merged, you can click the Split Cell button on the Tables And Borders toolbar.

Formatting a Table

In addition to formatting the table's data, you can also format the table's structure—for example, by adding borders and shading. In this section, you'll try your hand at both types of formatting.

The techniques for formatting table data are very similar to those for formatting regular slide text. Follow these steps to format the data in the sample table:

1. With the table heading selected, choose Table from the Format menu and click the Text Box tab to display these options:

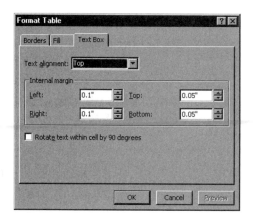

2. Click the arrow to the right of the Text Alignment edit box, choose Middle Centered from the drop-down list, and then click OK.

3. Next right-click the heading, choose Font from the shortcut menu, and change its size to 36 and its color to pink. Then click the Shadow check box and click OK.

4. Select all the data below the table heading, including the four column headings. Then click the arrow to the right of the Font Color button on the Drawing toolbar and select bright blue

from the drop-down palette. The data in the table will now be more legible against the slide's background.

5. Next select the Airfare, Hotel, and Transport column headings and the data below them. Choose Table from the Format menu. In the Format Table dialog box, click the Text Box tab, click the arrow to the right of the Text Alignment edit box, select Top Centered, and click OK. Click anywhere in the table to remove the selection and display these results:

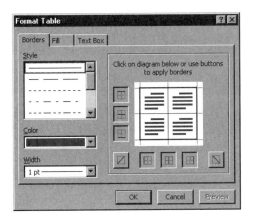

Typical Tour Package Prices

Paranormal Tours			
Tour	Airfare	Hotel	Transport
ET Exploration	$200	$475	$120
Ghostly B&Bs, US	$480	$695	$230
Ghostly B&Bs, Europe	$798	$1,350	$360
Bermuda Triangle	$566	$1,029	$345

To dress up a table or call attention to specific information, you can add borders or background shading (fills). Try this:

1. With the insertion point located anywhere in the active table, click the Table button and choose Select Table from the button's menu. Then choose Table from the Format menu. You see these options:

Adding a border

Removing a border ───────▶ The diagram on the right indicates that the table is surrounded by a border. To remove the border from any side of the table, you can turn off the appropriate button.

2. Change the Width setting to 3 pt. Then apply this change by clicking the outside borders of the diagram. Move the dialog box out of the way, click Preview to view your changes, and then click OK to return to the table.

3. Select the first row of the table (the row containing the table heading), right-click it, and choose Borders And Fill from the shortcut menu. On the Borders tab, select the 3 pt width, click the bottom border in the diagram, and then click OK.

4. Click anywhere outside the table to return to PowerPoint. If necessary, adjust the table's position and size (see the tip on page 105). Here's what the finished product looks like:

Typical Tour Package Prices

Paranormal Tours			
Tour	Airfare	Hotel	Transport
ET Exploration	$200	$475	$120
Ghostly B&Bs, US	$480	$695	$230
Ghostly B&Bs, Europe	$798	$1,350	$360
Bermuda Triangle	$566	$1,029	$345

7/1/99   Exotic Excursions   7

Using WordArt for Fancy Type Effects

The Paranormal Tours presentation is quite "presentable" as it is, but the title slide needs more attention-grabbing details. In earlier chapters, you learned how to create an impact by changing the font and size of the text on a slide. In this section, we'll introduce you to WordArt, which you can use to mold text into various shapes to fit the mood of the presentation or to flow around other elements on a slide.

Follow these steps to jazz up the title slide of the Paranormal Tours presentation:

1. Display the title slide of Paranormal Tours, click the title area, and then press the F2 key to select the title area rather than the title itself.

   Deleting the title area

2. Press the Delete key twice to remove the title and the area.

3. Click the Insert WordArt button on the Drawing toolbar to display this WordArt Gallery dialog box:

   The Insert WordArt button

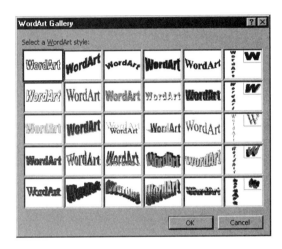

4. Click the second option in the last row and click OK to display this dialog box:

5. Type *Paranormal Tours* and click OK. A WordArt object in the shape you chose is embedded in the slide and the WordArt toolbar appears, as shown on the following page.

Obviously, a few adjustments to the text are in order. In addition to changing its position and size, you need to change its color. Here goes:

1. First dock the WordArt toolbar along the edge of the window by double-clicking its title bar.

The Format WordArt button

2. Click the Format WordArt button on the WordArt toolbar to display the dialog box shown here:

Editing WordArt objects

If you want to make changes to a WordArt object after you have embedded it in a slide, double-click the object to display both the WordArt toolbar and the Edit WordArt Text dialog box. You can then edit the text or use toolbar buttons to make adjustments. When you are finished, click outside the WordArt frame to return to PowerPoint.

3. Click the arrow to the right of the Color box and select the light blue box in the first row. Then click the Color box's arrow again and click Fill Effects to display this dialog box:

Changing the color of
WordArt text

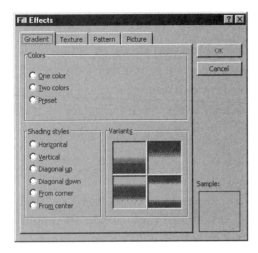

4. Click the One Color option in the Colors section of the Gradient tab and click OK twice. Now the color of the title stands out but coordinates with the rest of the slides in the Paranormal Tours presentation. (See the tip on page 114 for information about fill effects.)

5. Select the presenter's name and click the Align Right button on the Formatting toolbar.

6. Click the WordArt object to select it, and using its handles, reposition and resize the title text and object area until the slide looks something like this:

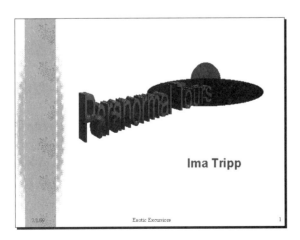

The WordArt toolbar

The WordArt toolbar comes with a variety of buttons you can use to change the look of WordArt text. To edit the text or change its font or size, click the WordArt Edit Text button. To change the style, simply click the WordArt Gallery button to redisplay its dialog box, and then select a new design. To change the color, size, or position, click the Format WordArt button. You can use the remaining buttons to alter the shape, rotation, letter height, orientation, alignment, and character spacing of the WordArt object. You can also change the object's shape by dragging its diamond-shaped *adjustment handle* in any direction. As you drag the handle, a dotted outline shows the approximate shape the object will assume when you release the mouse button.

7. Click anywhere outside the WordArt object to deselect it.

Using PowerPoint's Drawing Tools

So far you have used only a few of the buttons on the Drawing toolbar. In this section, we'll briefly discuss some of the tools you can use to draw graphic objects on slides. A detailed discussion of all the drawing tools is beyond the scope of this book, so we'll show you a simple example and then leave you to explore on your own. Before you start drawing, let's set up the screen like this:

1. With Slide 1 displayed in slide view, choose Ruler from the View menu to display the rulers.

Displaying guides

2. Choose Guides from the expanded View menu to display horizontal and vertical lines that will help you position your drawings. Your screen now looks like this:

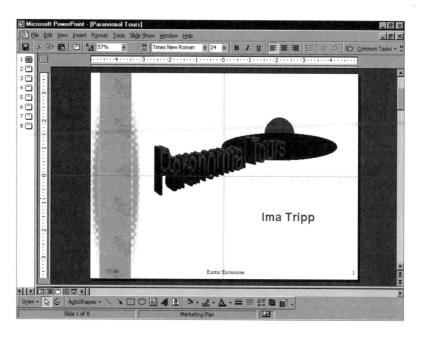

You can drag each guide to position it where you need it. As you drag, the guide's distance from the corresponding ruler's zero mark—zero is the center—is displayed so that you can use the guide to precisely position objects on the slide. For example, to position a rectangle so that its top and bottom edges are exactly 1 inch above and 2 inches below a slide's center, you would drag the horizontal guide to the 1-inch mark above the zero on the vertical ruler and draw the rectangle from the guide to approximately the 2-inch mark below the zero on the vertical ruler. Then you would drag the horizontal guide to the 2-inch mark and align the bottom edge of the rectangle with the guide. To add guides, you hold down the Ctrl key as you grab a displayed guide. The original guide remains stationary as you drag a new guide. To place the new guide, you release the mouse button and then release the Ctrl key. To remove a guide, you can simply drag it off the slide.

Adding and removing guides

You can draw a number of basic shapes, including lines, rectangles, and squares, using the tools on the Drawing toolbar. To get a feel for drawing shapes and working with the Drawing toolbar, let's replace the UFO graphic on the title slide of the Paranormal Tours presentation with a "black hole":

1. With Slide 1 still displayed, select the UFO and press the Delete key.

The Oval button

2. Click the Oval button on the Drawing toolbar and position the cross-hair pointer at the right end of the Paranormal Tours title. Hold down the left mouse button and drag to the right and down until the oval is about 3 inches high and 2 inches wide. (Remember to use the guides.) The oval should obscure the last few letters of the title text, like this:

Ima Tripp

Exotic Excursions

The Fill Color button

The Line Color button

3. With the oval selected (surrounded by handles), click the arrow to the right of the Fill Color button on the Drawing toolbar, and select Fill Effects to display the dialog box shown earlier on page 111.

4. Click the One Color option and then change the color to dark blue. Select Horizontal in the Shading Styles section and select the bottom right graphic option in the Variants section. Then click OK.

5. Next click the arrow to the right of the Line Color button on the Drawing toolbar, and select No Line from the top of the palette to remove the border surrounding the oval. (Alternatively, you could make the border blend with the object by making it dark blue.)

6. Click the Draw button and then choose Order and Send Backward. The oval no longer obscures the title text.

7. Use the mouse (and the guides) to resize the oval and the WordArt object so that the oval is centered over the last three letters of the title.

8. Click a blank area of the slide to deselect any objects.

9. Turn off the rulers and the guides so you can see the results at the top of the facing page.

Other fill options

In addition to changing the gradient shading pattern of an object in the Fill Effects dialog box, you can also change the texture and pattern on their respective tabs. (We discuss these two tabs on page 123.) On the Picture tab, you can click the Select Picture button and select a picture file created in another program (such as Paint), as the fill for an object.

Rotating, flipping, and aligning objects

You can use the Free Rotate button on the Drawing toolbar or the Free Rotate command on the Rotate Or Flip submenu of the Draw menu to rotate an object about its center. Simply select the object, click the toolbar button or choose the command, point to one of the object's corner handles, and drag to the left or right. If you want to rotate an object exactly 90 degrees to the left or right, select the object and then choose the appropriate command from the Rotate Or Flip submenu of the Draw menu. To flip objects horizontally or vertically, select the object and choose the equivalent command from the Rotate Or Flip submenu. Finally, you can align several objects on a slide in various ways. Select the objects (hold down the Shift key as you click each object), choose Align Or Distribute from the Draw menu, and then choose one of the commands from the submenu.

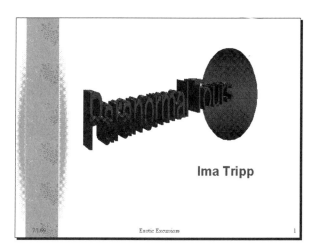

With all of the resources supplied by PowerPoint, you shouldn't have any trouble adding visual appeal to your presentations. Just remember to keep it simple; otherwise, your audience might start paying more attention to your artwork than to the content of your presentation.

5
Creating a Custom Template

We show you how to design your own template by using PowerPoint's masters. As you create the template, you change the font, add a graphic to the background, and alter the color scheme. Then you apply the custom template to an existing presentation.

Students presenting a report to their class, employees introducing a new concept to their department, or anyone wishing to add their own touch to a presentation will find custom templates invaluable.

Template created and concepts covered:

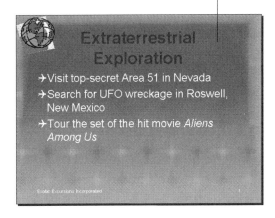

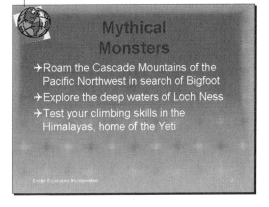

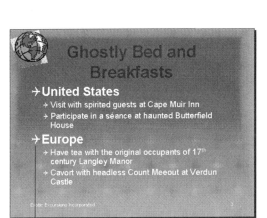

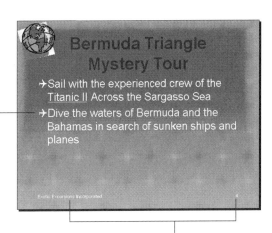

PowerPoint provides a wide variety of design templates to choose from, but you aren't limited to those templates. You can create your own, either by modifying an existing template or by designing a new one from scratch. In this chapter, we show you how to create a brand new template, with the fonts, bullet characters, color scheme, and so on, of your own choosing. Then you apply the new template to an existing presentation so that you can see how a custom template looks in action.

Designing a Template

Before you start a new template, you need to ask yourself a few simple questions. For example, what kind of message or feeling do you want the template to convey? Should the template have a formal or informal look? What sort of design elements do you want to include? After you've sorted out the answers to these questions, you can begin working on the actual template design.

Corporate templates

The advent of presentation programs has greatly simplified the task of creating presentations. Many companies no longer need special departments to handle the making of slides, overhead transparencies, and so on because almost anyone can quickly put together a presentation. To ensure the quality and consistency of the presentations delivered on their behalf, large companies are now developing corporate templates that every employee should use. Logos, special colors, and fonts are often included in these templates to give them a corporate look. Before you spend a lot of time developing your own templates, you might want to check that you will be allowed to use them.

For the purposes of this chapter, you want to create a template that can be applied to the Sample Tours presentation. Because the presentation's topic is travel (in other words, recreation), a relaxed, less formal look is probably the best choice. You can also play off the subject of the paranormal by using colors and shading that invoke a feeling of mystery and suspense.

With these decisions out of the way, you need to open a new, blank presentation. You won't actually create slides for this presentation, however. Instead, you'll use its blank template as a basis for creating your own template. Follow these steps:

1. Start PowerPoint. When the PowerPoint dialog box appears, double-click the Blank Presentation option to open the New Slide dialog box.

2. Double-click the Title Slide autolayout. PowerPoint displays a blank slide with nothing other than title and subtitle areas with placeholder text.

Before you start creating your template, take a moment to read the following section on masters, which are an integral part of the template design process.

Using Masters

As their name suggests, masters are the mechanism by which a template controls the formatting of a presentation's slides. Although you want your presentations to be attractive, you don't want the look of the slides to be more memorable than the message. One sure way to distract an audience is to vary the look of a presentation from slide to slide. By using masters as the foundation for a template, you can ensure that all the slides to which the template is applied have consistent fonts, backgrounds, and color schemes. Masters also provide an easy way to make across-the-board changes to the look of your presentations. PowerPoint 2000 has four masters:

- The *title master.* Controls the formatting of the title slides.

- The *slide master.* Controls the formatting of all other slide types.

- The *notes master.* Controls the formatting of speakers' notes.

- The *handout master.* Controls the formatting of handouts you prepare for your audience.

In this chapter, you'll work with the slide master. (See the tips below for more information about the other types of masters.)

Formatting the title master

The techniques for creating and formatting the title master are the same as those for the slide master. To create a new title master, first switch to master view by choosing Master and then Slide Master from the View menu. Then choose New Title Master from the Insert menu. To return to the title master later, choose Master and then Title Master from the View menu.

Formatting the notes master

To customize the look of speaker's notes, activate the notes master by choosing Master and Notes Master from the View menu. Use the notes master to add headers, footers, the date, and slide number to your speaker's notes, and to customize the bulleted items for your notes.

Formatting the handout master

To get an idea of how handouts will look when printed, display the handout master by choosing Master and then Handout Master from the View menu. (You can also hold down the Shift key and click the Slide Sorter View button.) The slides are represented by boxes with dashed lines. Use the buttons on the Handout Master toolbar to change the setup of the pages.

Formatting the Slide Master

With that discussion out of the way, you're ready to begin creating a template. Because the Sample Tours presentation has no title slide, you'll work only with the slide master. Bear in mind, however, that the techniques we'll discuss can also be used to format the title master.

Changing the Font

In Chapter 3, we showed you how to change the size and style of text using the Formatting toolbar. In this section, you will use the Font dialog box. Although the toolbar provides quick access to different font effects, the Font dialog box offers a wider range of effects, including superscript, subscript, and embossing. Follow these steps to change the font of the slide master:

Displaying the slide master

1. Switch to slide view. Then choose Master and Slide Master from the View menu. Your screen now looks like this:

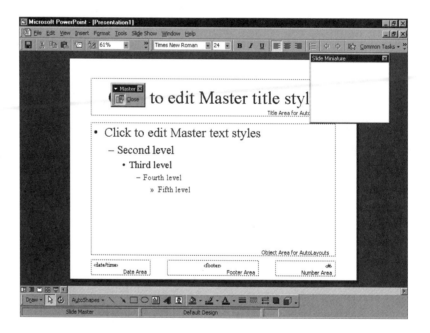

As you can see, the slide master is divided into several areas. We discuss each of these areas as you progress through the chapter. For now, take a moment to study the slide master and then move on to the next step.

2. Close the Master toolbar and then close the Slide Miniature window.

3. Click the title area on the slide master and choose Font from the Format menu to display the Font dialog box shown here:

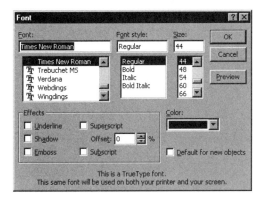

4. Select Arial in the Font list, Bold in the Font Style list, and 48 in the Size list. Then click OK.

5. Next click the object area on the slide master, select the text of the first bulleted item, and change the setting in the Font box on the Formatting toolbar to Arial.

6. The Sample Tours presentation has two bullet levels, so select the text of the Second Level subordinate item and then repeat step 5. Here are the results:

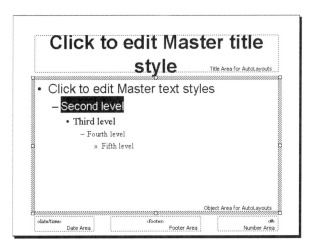

Repositioning and resizing slide areas

As you know, you can reposition the title or object area of a slide by dragging it, and you can resize it by dragging its handles. Keep in mind that when you resize an area of a slide, the text inside it wraps to fit the area's new size. As an example, a single line of text in a title area might wrap to two lines if you decrease the area's size. You can control whether text wraps or not by first selecting the area and choosing Placeholder from the Format menu. When the Format AutoShape dialog box appears, click the Text Box tab, deselect or select the Word Wrap Text In AutoShape check box, and click OK. If you turn text wrapping off by deselecting this option, any text that does not fit within the area's frame continues beyond the frame's borders and, if necessary, even beyond the edges of the slide. Notice that you can also change the positioning of text within the box, adjust margins, and rotate the text 90° by selecting options in the Format Auto-Shape dialog box.

Saving the Template

Well, you still have quite a bit of design work to do, but before you go any further, you should save the slide master as a template to safeguard your changes. You'll store the template in the Presentation Designs folder, where PowerPoint's other templates are located. Follow these steps:

1. Choose Save As from the File menu. When the Save As dialog box appears, click the arrow to the right of the Save As Type box and select Design Template.

2. Check that the setting in the Save In box is Templates. (By default, PowerPoint saves custom design templates in the C:\Windows\Application Data\Microsoft\Templates folder.)

3. In the File Name edit box, type *Travel* as the name of the custom template and then click Save.

As with any PowerPoint presentation, from now on you can simply click the Save button to save any changes you make to the new template. (And although we don't explicitly tell you to, you should save your work often.)

Creating a Background

All the templates that ship with PowerPoint have colored patterns and some sort of graphic gracing their backgrounds. You can create a background with specific colors, patterns, textures, and so on, by using PowerPoint's Background command. You can also use this command to add a graphic to the background (see the tip on page 124). Let's create a background for the Travel template now:

The Templates folder

When you save a design template in the default folder, you can not only apply the design to any presentation (see page 133), but you can also create a brand new presentation based on the design template. Choose New from the File menu and on the General tab of the New Presentation dialog box, simply double-click the template's name.

1. With the slide master for the Travel template displayed, choose Background from the Format menu to display this dialog box:

As you can see, PowerPoint supplies the ready-made color scheme, shown in the sample slide in the Background Fill section of the dialog box. Currently, the background of the slide is white. (If you were to add a graph, its markers would have the colors shown in the sample graph.)

2. Click the arrow to the right of the blank edit box in the Background Fill section to display this drop-down list of options:

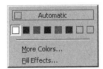

Changing the background color

3. Change the background color by selecting the seventh of the eight boxes in the color-scheme row (lilac, in this case). The background of the sample slide instantly changes. Now click the Preview button and notice that the color of the slide master's background has changed as well. (If the Background dialog box blocks your view, you can drag its title bar to move the dialog box out of your way.)

4. Click the arrow to the right of the Background Fill edit box again, select the Fill Effects option, and then click the Pattern tab to display these options:

Adding a background pattern

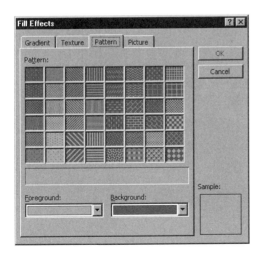

5. Select a pattern option in the Pattern section and notice the effect in the Sample box at the bottom of the dialog box.

6. Experiment with some of the other patterns and then click the Texture tab to display these options:

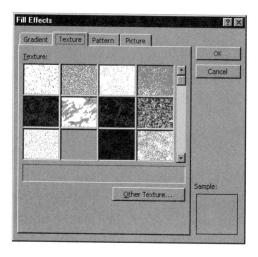

7. Experiment with some of the texture options and then click the Cancel button.

Already you can get a feel for the range of background possibilities that PowerPoint has to offer. As you'll see as you follow these steps, you can also customize the color:

1. With the Background dialog box still open on your screen, select the More Colors option from the Background Fill dropdown list. The Colors dialog box appears, displaying the slide master's current background color.

2. Click the Custom tab to display these options:

Using a graphic as the background

To use a graphic as your background for slides, click the Picture tab of the Fill Effects dialog box. Then click the Select Picture button to display the Select Picture dialog box, browse to the location of the picture file you want to use, and double-click the filename. Next click OK twice to close the Select Picture and Fill Effects dialog boxes. Click Apply or Apply To All to close the Background dialog box. PowerPoint then uses the graphic to fill the slide background.

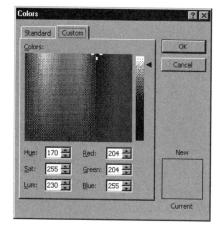

3. Half-hidden at the top of the Colors box is a cross hair. Point to it and drag it anywhere in the box. When you release the mouse button, PowerPoint displays the color you've selected in the New box; analyzes its red, green, and blue content, as well as its hue, saturation, and luminance (intensity); and identifies the luminance on the vertical scale to the right of the Colors box.

4. Now point to the arrow to the right of the vertical luminance scale, and drag it up and down, noting the changes in the New box and in the Lum, Red, Green, and Blue boxes.

◄─────────────── Changing color intensity

5. Take a little time to explore the Colors dialog box further. Then when you're ready to move on, use the arrows at the end of their boxes to change the settings for hue, saturation, and luminance to reflect the numbers shown here:

Hue   155
Sat(uration)   165
Lum(inance)   155

As you enter each new setting, notice that the positions of the cross hair and the luminance scale arrow change, as do the settings in the Red, Green, and Blue boxes and the color in the New box.

6. Click OK to return to the Background dialog box.

Before you apply the new color to the slide master, let's include a bit of shading, just for added interest:

1. Select the Fill Effects option from the Background Fill drop-down list to display the Gradient tab of the Fill Effects dialog box, shown earlier on page 111.

◄─────────────── Adding shading

2. Select One Color in the Colors section and From Title in the Shading Styles section. Then click the second box in the Variants section and click OK.

3. Click Apply to apply the new color and shading to the slide master of the Travel template. The results are shown on the next page.

Changing hue and saturation

When you create a custom color in PowerPoint, you can change its hue by dragging the cross hair horizontally across the Colors box. To change the saturation, drag the cross hair vertically.

Adding a Graphic to the Background

You can use the Background command to make a graphic the entire background of a slide or template (see the tip on page 124). If you want a graphic to occupy only part of the background, you must use the techniques we discussed in Chapter 2 instead. For the Travel template, let's insert a clip art graphic from the Clip Gallery and then resize and reposition it as appropriate for the background. (We assume that you've read Chapter 2 and are familiar with the Clip Gallery.) Here goes:

1. With the Travel template displayed in slide master view, click the Insert Clip Art button on the Drawing toolbar.

2. When the Clip Gallery window appears, type *world* in the Search For Clips edit box and then press Enter.

3. Select the three-dimensional globe graphic in the third to last row and click Insert Clip from the drop-down button palette that appears. Then close the Clip Gallery window.

4. Select the graphic and drag its corner handles inward until it is about 1½ inches in height and width. (You can display the rulers and use them as a guide.) Then point anywhere inside the graphic and drag it to the top left corner of the slide master.

5. With the graphic still selected, click the Draw button on the Drawing toolbar and choose Order and then Send To Back so that the graphic does not obscure the slide title.

6. Next deselect the graphic by clicking anywhere on the slide. As shown here, the graphic appears "behind" the title text:

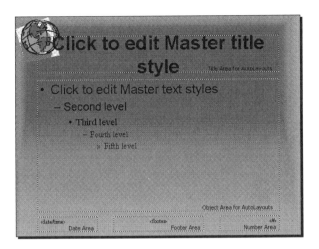

Changing the Bullet Character

Although changing the bullet character might not be quite as dramatic as altering the color scheme or adding a graphic, it can have an impact on the overall look of your presentation. PowerPoint offers a wide variety of bullet characters for you to choose from, as you'll see when you follow these steps:

1. With the Travel template open in slide master view, right-click the first bulleted item. Choose Bullets And Numbering from the shortcut menu to display the dialog box shown here:

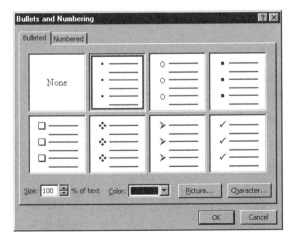

2. Click the Character button to display the dialog box shown on the next page.

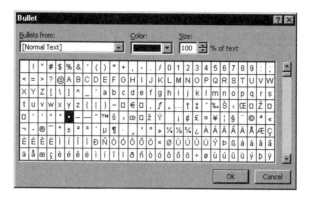

By default, PowerPoint uses one of the 256 characters that make up the font you are using for the text of bulleted items, which is designated as Normal Text

Selecting a new character

3. Click the arrow to the right of the Bullets From box and select Wingdings from the drop-down list.

4. Select a symbol that you think would be appropriate for a bullet character. (We selected the airplane symbol in the second row of the Wingdings palette.)

5. Click OK to return to the slide master with the new character in place for all bulleted item levels.

Changing the bullet character's size

6. Open the Bullets And Numbering dialog box again, double-click *100* in the Size box, type *80* to reduce the size of the bullet character a bit, and click OK to return to the slide master. Here are the results after you deselect the object area:

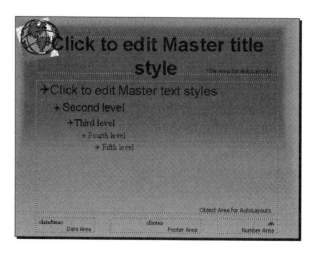

Adding a Footer and a Slide Number

At the bottom of the slide master, you may have noticed three boxes labeled Date Area, Footer Area, and Number Area. Information you enter in these boxes is added to each slide in the presentation. By default, the boxes sit at the bottom of the slide master but you can move them to any part of the slide. Follow these steps to add a footer and a slide number:

1. Click the slide master's Date Area box to select it. (PowerPoint surrounds the box with handles and a shaded border.) Press the Delete key to delete the box.

   Deleting an area box from the master slide

2. Click the Footer Area box, click the arrow to the right of the Zoom box on the Standard toolbar, and select 100%. You can now see the footer area more clearly.

3. Click the <footer> placeholder. (This placeholder won't appear on the slide even though it shows up on the slide master.) Type *Exotic Excursions Incorporated* and click the Align Left button.

   Adding the slide number is a bit trickier. You must use the Header And Footer command, as these steps illustrate:

1. Scroll the slide to the right, click the Number Area box to select it, and choose Header And Footer from the View menu. PowerPoint displays this Header And Footer dialog box:

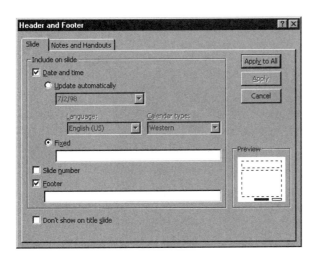

2. Select the Slide Number check box and click Apply To All.

Inserting the date, time, and slide number

You can insert the date, time, and/or slide number on a specific slide by displaying the slide and choosing Header And Footer from the View menu. Select the appropriate options in the dialog box and then click Apply. The option(s) you selected appear only on the current slide. To display the date, time, and/or slide number on every slide in a presentation, click the Apply To All button in the Header And Footer dialog box.

3. Now switch to slide view to check the footer and slide number. If necessary, turn off the rulers and then select Fit from the bottom of the Zoom drop-down list to see the entire slide.

Everything looks pretty good, but you should shift the footer to the bottom left corner of the slide to create balance. While you're at it, change the font of both the footer and the slide number to correspond with the title and bulleted text font by following these steps:

1. Switch to slide master view by holding down the Shift key and clicking the Slide View button.

Repositioning the footer

2. Select the Footer Area box and drag it to the left, to the position previously occupied by the Date Area box. As you drag, be careful to keep the top of the Footer Area box aligned with the top of the Number Area box. (If you have trouble positioning the box, try clicking the Draw button on the Drawing toolbar, choosing Nudge, and then choosing the appropriate direction command.)

Changing the footer and slide number font

3. With the Footer Area box still selected, select the footer text and select Arial from the Font drop-down list on the Formatting toolbar.

4. Next select the slide number placeholder (<#>) in the Number Area box and repeat step 3 for the slide number. (If you have trouble seeing the placeholders, use the Zoom drop-down list to increase the magnification.) Here's what the slide master looks like now:

Adjusting dates, footers, and slide numbers

If you want to change the location of a slide's date, footer, or slide number, switch to slide master view. Then select the Date Area, Footer Area, or Number Area box, and drag it to a new location on the slide master. To increase or decrease the size of any box, drag its handles in the appropriate direction.

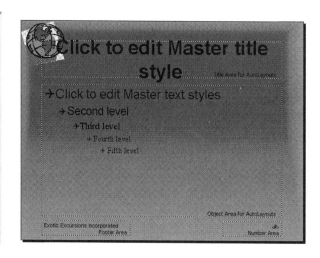

Changing the Color Scheme

Before you put your template to the test, you need to make one more significant change. As you've already seen, the color of the text makes it difficult to read against the background color you selected. Using the Font dialog box to change the text color would be tedious because you would have to work with each individual line of text. Instead, you can use the Slide Color Scheme dialog box to change all the text at once. Here's how:

1. Right-click the slide master outside the title and object areas and choose Slide Color Scheme from the shortcut menu.

2. In the Color Scheme dialog box, click the Custom tab to display these options:

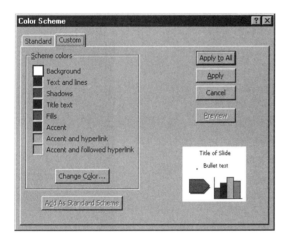

The boxes in the Scheme Colors section of the dialog box depict the colors of the various elements on the current slide. (Because you changed the background color using the Custom Background dialog box, the current background color is not reflected here.) As you'll see in a moment, you can click an element's color box and then click the Change Color button to alter all occurrences of that element. The table at the top of the next page describes the elements affected by the eight color boxes.

Ready-made color schemes

The Standard tab of the Color Scheme dialog box has a number of ready-made color schemes for your presentations. (The color schemes vary depending on the template that is currently in use.) If you want to apply one of these color schemes to your presentation, double-click it. To apply a color scheme to the current slide only, select the scheme and then click Apply. You don't want to bombard your audience with a plethora of color, so exercise caution when you apply different color schemes to different slides (see the tip on page 133).

The slide elements

Color box	Affected elements
Background	Slide background
Text And Lines	Bulleted text, text entered in a box created with the Text Box drawing tool, lines and arrows drawn with the Line drawing tool, and the outlines for AutoShapes and objects drawn with any of the drawing tools
Shadows	Shadows created with the Shadow drawing tool
Title Text	Slide titles
Fills	Interior of AutoShapes and objects drawn with the drawing tools and the first color in graphs
Accent	Second color in graphs, organization charts, and other added elements
Accent And Hyperlink	Third color in graphs, organization charts, and other added elements (including hyperlinks)
Accent And Followed Hyperlink	Fourth color in graphs, organization charts, and other added elements (including followed hyperlinks)

Changing the text and line color

3. Next click the Text And Lines box, and then click the Change Color button to display the Text And Line Color dialog box shown here:

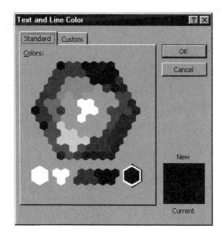

Designating a standard scheme

After you develop your own color scheme you can save it with the current presentation. Click the Add As Standard Scheme button on the Custom tab of the Color Scheme dialog box. PowerPoint adds the new color scheme to the Standard tab. Then whenever you open the corresponding presentation, your custom color scheme is available for use. (To delete the scheme, select it on the Standard tab and then click the Delete Scheme button.)

4. Select the White hexagon in the bottom left corner of the Standard tab (below the color palette) and click OK. When you return to the Color Scheme dialog box, notice that the Text And Lines box is now white.

5. Next click the Title Text box and click the Change Color button.

6. When the Title Text Color dialog box appears, click the Custom tab to display options similar to those in the Colors dialog box shown on page 124.

7. Change the Hue, Sat(uration), and Lum(inance) settings so that they read as specified below. (Drag the cross hair in the Colors box and drag the luminance scale arrow. You can also use the arrows at the end of each box or enter the numbers directly to change the settings.)

Hue	196
Sat(uration)	140
Lum(inance)	160

8. Click OK to return to the Color Scheme dialog box, where the Title Text color box is now purple.

9. Finally, click the Apply button to apply the new color scheme to the slide master.

If you were working with the slides of an actual presentation, rather than a slide master, you would click the Apply To All button to apply the new color scheme to all the slides of the presentation.

Although you made only a couple of changes to the color scheme of the Travel template, you were careful to select colors that complemented one another. Before you start creating color schemes on your own, be sure to read the adjacent tip about the effect of color.

Applying a Custom Template

After all that work, you're probably anxious to apply your custom template to the Sample Tours presentation. Before you do, however, bear in mind the following: because you are applying the template to a set of preexisting slides, you might have to make a few minor adjustments, such as repositioning the title or object area. Usually these adjustments won't be necessary if you select a template first and then add text to your slides. Nonetheless, we'll walk you through any changes that have to be made. Follow the steps on the next page to put the custom template to the test.

The effect of color

The colors you use in your presentations are just as important as the fonts you use. Like fonts, different colors can send different messages to your audience. For example, "cool" colors such as green, blue, and violet are associated with oceans and pastoral settings and can imply peace and tranquillity. "Warm" colors such as red, orange, and yellow, on the other hand, are associated with fire and can imply aggression and intensity. You also need to be aware of these factors when selecting colors for a presentation:

- Use cool colors, which tend to recede from the audience, as background colors. Use warm colors, which tend to advance, to call attention to specific items.

- Similarly, use bright colors to visually advance an element. Muted or darker colors will recede.

- When creating electronic slides, use a dark background. For transparencies and for 35mm slides, use a light background.

- Avoid placing red and green next to each other. (People who are color-blind may not be able to distinguish between them.)

- Use color to highlight data. For example, format positive numbers in blue and choose red for negative numbers.

- Select color to focus attention on a few key areas. Too many colors together can distract your audience.

1. With the Travel template open in slide master view, click the Save button and then choose Close from the File menu.

2. Click the Open button. In the Open dialog box, change Files Of Type to Presentations And Shows, click My Documents in the shortcuts bar, and double-click Sample Tours.

3. Click the Common Tasks button on the Formatting toolbar and choose Apply Design Template from the drop-down menu.

4. Scroll the list of templates in the Apply Design Template dialog box, select Travel (note the sample in the preview box), and then click Apply. Here's what Slide 1 looks like now:

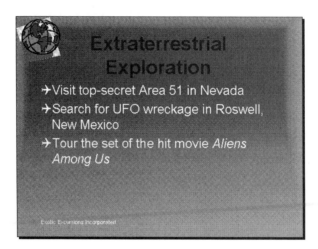

5. Save the presentation with the new template in place.

Fine-Tuning

As we mentioned earlier, you may have to make a few adjustments to the Sample Tours presentation after the new template is applied. Take a moment now to scroll through the slides of the presentation. Notice anything wrong? Well, for starters, the slide number may be missing from your slides. If so, follow these steps:

Displaying the slide numbers

1. With Slide 1 of Sample Tours displayed in slide view, choose Header And Footer from the View menu.

2. When the Header And Footer dialog box appears, select the Slide Number check box and click Apply To All.

3. Now scroll through the slides to check the placement of titles, bulleted text, footers, and so on.

4. The title of Slide 2 is the only one that doesn't wrap to two lines. For consistency, click an insertion point to the right of the *l* in *Mythical*, press Shift+Enter, and then press Delete to remove the space before *Monsters*.

5. Before you move on to the next chapter, check out your work in slide sorter view. If everything looks good, give yourself a pat on the back for a job well done!

6. Save and close the presentation.

   Now you can put your skills and creative energy to work designing your own templates.

More About Electronic Presentations

After a survey of equipment needs, we discuss ways of adding interaction, such as branching to another presentation. Then you learn more about delivering electronic slide shows, including setting up your presentation on a computer that doesn't have PowerPoint.

The skills gained here will ensure the smooth delivery of any presentation, including the times when travel is necessary, such as for sales meetings, fundraising efforts, or educational conferences.

Tasks performed and concepts covered:

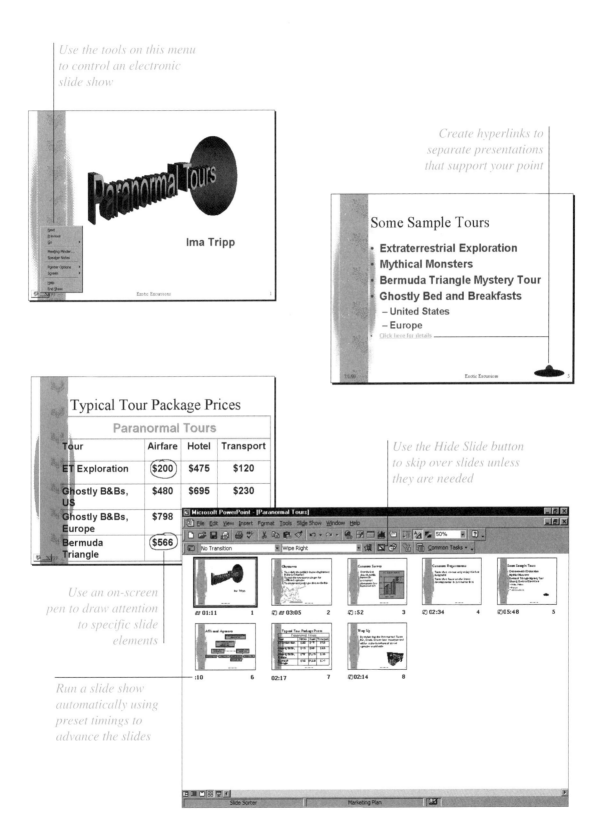

Use the tools on this menu to control an electronic slide show

Create hyperlinks to separate presentations that support your point

Use the Hide Slide button to skip over slides unless they are needed

Use an on-screen pen to draw attention to specific slide elements

Run a slide show automatically using preset timings to advance the slides

In Chapter 1, we demonstrated how to run an electronic slide show from your computer. In this chapter, we first discuss equipment needs and the logistics of preparing for a presentation. Then we show you some of the more sophisticated things you can do with electronic slide shows. To round out the chapter, we cover how to take your slide shows on the road.

Electronic slide shows take more thought to prepare than transparencies and 35mm slides—at least, the first slide show does—because you need to carefully consider the hardware aspects of the presentation. With transparencies and 35mm slides, you usually show up for a presentation with a folder of acetate sheets or a carousel of slides, ready to dim the lights and get right to the point. Things aren't quite so simple with an electronic slide show. For one thing, the type of equipment you use varies with the size and nature of your audience and for another, the potential exists for something to be missing or incompatible. For this reason, we start this section with a quick look at what you need in the way of hardware to give a successful electronic slide show.

Equipment for Electronic Slide Shows

The first thing to consider when you decide to develop an electronic slide show is how you plan to deliver the presentation. Will you be making the presentation on your own computer or someone else's? Will the audience be coming to you, will you be doing the traveling, or will you simply post the presentation on an Internet server so that people can view it on their own time?

Whenever possible, it is wise to control as many variables as you can by developing the presentation on the type of computer that will be used to deliver or view the slide show. Otherwise, you can spend hours fine-tuning a dynamic presentation only to find all that hard work wasted.

The next question to consider is the size of the audience. Will you be making the presentation to a cozy group of less than 5 people around a conference table, a seminar of 30 people, an

Which computer and where?

Size of audience

auditorium of 100 or more, or will each person be viewing the presentation on their own computer? In the latter case, you don't have to worry about special equipment; otherwise, you need to ensure that your presentation's slides are large enough to be easily viewed by everyone. Although an intimate group might not mind crowding around a regular computer screen, for larger groups you will need a larger image. If you don't want to dim the lights and curtail audience interaction, you could use a 20-inch or larger monitor for a small seminar. But for addressing a room full of people, you will need either an LCD panel or an LCD projector to get your message across clearly.

An LCD panel is a flat screen that plugs into a computer and displays a duplicate of the image you see on the computer's monitor. You lay the panel on an overhead projector to cast that image onto a standard slide screen. The resolution of the image is determined by the type of panel and by the brightness of the overhead projector. An active matrix panel with an overhead projector of 3000 to 4000 lumens is quite adequate for an audience of 50 or more people. Even with the highest resolution, though, the colors projected with the panel may not be the same as those on the computer's screen, so it's best not to use LCD panels in situations where precise colors are important. (Fashion design and interior decorating are good examples.) An LCD projector operates on a similar principle, except that a light source and lens are built into the hardware. A good projector can project clear images for an audience of up to 300 people, but high quality projectors with active matrix displays and other image-enhancing features are expensive. Lower quality projectors cost less but may produce poor images that do nothing but annoy audiences.

For occasional use, you might be better off renting the necessary equipment, but then you need to be careful that all cables and other accessories are included with the primary hardware. If you are renting locally and transporting the equipment to the presentation site, you'll want to put everything together and test for compatibility before you leave, allowing time to return to the rental company for missing or replacement parts if necessary. If someone else is in charge of setting up the

LCD panels

LCD projectors

Adjusting for the presentation output

When you change the output type for a presentation in the Page Setup dialog box, some of the elements that you define in one output type may shift when you display them in the new output type. For example, a graph may no longer be correctly sized for its slide after you switch output types from 35mm Slides to On-Screen Show. Always check every slide and make any necessary adjustments after you change the output type.

equipment, you should check with him or her ahead of time to prevent any misunderstandings about equipment needs.

Having passed on those few nuggets of wisdom, which we learned the hard way, let's fire up PowerPoint and talk more about creating and running electronic slide shows.

Using the Slide Show Tools

To help you control an electronic slide show, PowerPoint provides a variety of tools. As mentioned in Chapter 1, moving the mouse pointer during a slide show displays a button in the bottom left corner that you can click to open a menu of these tools. (You can also right-click to display the tools' shortcut menu.) For example, by clicking the button and choosing the Go command, you can jump directly to a specific slide in the presentation. Let's spend a few moments getting familiar with some of the slide show tools:

1. Open Paranormal Tours and switch to slide show view. Then click the mouse button to display the speaker's name.

2. Move the mouse pointer over the screen, and when the slide show button appears in the bottom left corner, click it once to display this menu:

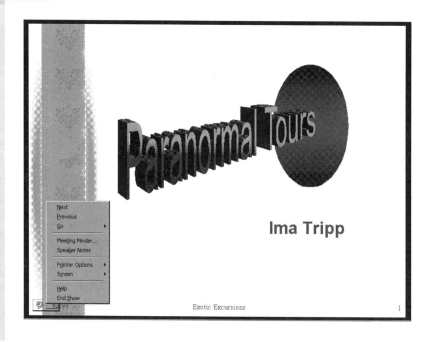

Meeting tools

When you run an electronic slide show during a meeting, you can rely on PowerPoint's Meeting Minder to help you record minutes or jot down action items. Simply choose Meeting Minder from the Slide Show shortcut menu and use the tabs in the Meeting Minder dialog box. Any information you enter on the Meeting Minutes tab can then be viewed via the Meeting Minder dialog box or by exporting the information to a Word document. When you record action items on the Action Items tab, PowerPoint adds an Action Items slide to the end of your presentation so that you and your colleagues can review the items. Like the meeting minutes, you can also export information on the Action Items tab to a Word document. To export minutes or action items to Word, click the Export button at the bottom of the Meeting Minder dialog box, select an export option, and then click Export Now. To take notes as you progress through a slide show, choose Speaker Notes from the Slide Show shortcut menu. If you type notes in the Speaker Notes dialog box, PowerPoint adds the notes to the presentation's notes pages. View the notes by switching to notes pages view or by opening the Speaker Notes dialog box during the slide show.

3. Choose Next to move to the next slide in the presentation.

4. Press Page Up once to remove the title and then press Page Up again to move back to the first slide.

Retracing your steps

5. Right-click the slide and choose Go and then Slide Navigator to display this dialog box:

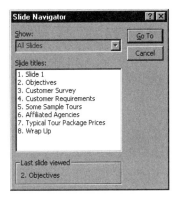

As you can see, PowerPoint identifies each slide by its number and its title. Because the title of the active slide is a WordArt object, it's listed simply as Slide 1.

6. Select Some Sample Tours, the fifth slide in the presentation, and click the Go To button to jump to Slide 5. Then if necessary, click the mouse button until you have built the slide's bulleted list.

Jumping to another slide

7. Right-click again and choose Pointer Options and then Hidden from the menu. The mouse pointer disappears.

Hiding the mouse pointer

8. Press Page Down to move to Slide 6.

9. Press Ctrl+A to redisplay the pointer. (You can also right-click and choose Pointer Options and then Arrow from the menu.)

Redisplaying the mouse pointer

10. Right-click a final time and choose End Show to exit slide show view.

Running a Presentation Automatically

As you've already seen, you can manually run a slide show from your computer, clicking mouse buttons or pressing keys to progress from one slide to the next. But what if you want to move around the room as you deliver a presentation, or you want to be able to set the presentation in motion and then forget about it, as with point-of-purchase presentations? Instead of being tied to a mouse or keyboard, you can set up the slide show to automatically move from one slide to another. Let's automate the Paranormal Tours presentation:

1. Switch to slide sorter view, select 50% in the Zoom drop-down list, and choose Select All from the Edit menu to select all the slides in the presentation.

2. Click the Slide Transition button on the Slide Sorter toolbar to display the Slide Transition dialog box shown on page 80. (You've already used the options in the Effect section of the dialog box to apply transitions and set their speed.)

Setting the slide timings

3. Click the Automatically After check box in the Advance section and enter *00:10* (10 seconds) in the highlighted edit box. (You can also use the Up arrow button until it displays 00:10.) Then click Apply To All. PowerPoint indicates the timings you have set below each slide, as shown here:

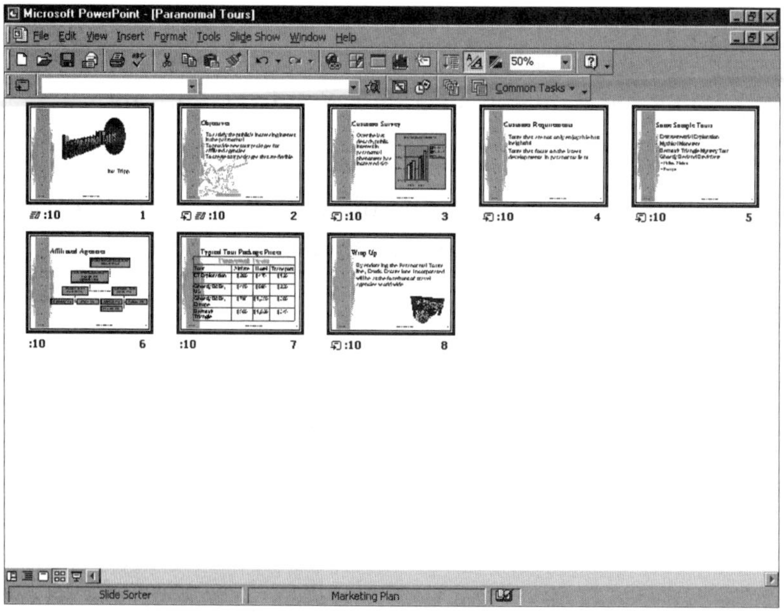

Your slides may have different combinations of transition and build icons, depending on the experimenting you have done with the techniques described on page 80.

4. Now choose Set Up Show from the Slide Show menu to display this dialog box:

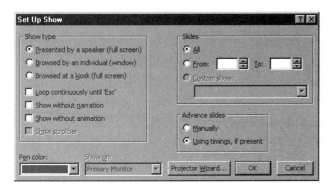

5. In the Advance Slides section, check that the Using Timings, If Present option is selected and click OK.

6. Choose View Show from the Slide Show menu. PowerPoint switches to slide show view and displays Slide 1. After 10 seconds, it displays the speaker's name. Then PowerPoint advances to Slide 2, and so on.

7. Interrupt the show at any time by pressing Esc to return to slide sorter view.

Preparing Speaker-Controlled Presentations

The title of this section might surprise you. After all, aren't all presentations delivered by speakers? Not anymore. Presentation programs like PowerPoint now incorporate stand-alone capabilities that you can use to produce self-running presentations. You can mail these presentations to clients or use them as point-of-purchase displays or at trade shows. However, the majority of presentations are still delivered by a live human being. In this section, we will cover some of the special effects that can be incorporated into a speaker-controlled electronic slide show. We'll also discuss how to rehearse for a presentation.

Adding Interaction

One measure of a good presentation is how well it delivers its message—whether it gets its point across. The design of the

More about the Set Up Show command

In the Show Type section of the Set Up Show dialog box, you can designate the type of slide show you want to set up. For a speaker-delivered presentation, leave the first option selected. For a self-running presentation (such as at a kiosk), select the second or third option. You can also set up the presentation to loop continuously until you press Esc, and you can run the presentation without narration or animation. If you want to show only specific slides during a slide show, enter the numbers of the slides in the From and To edit boxes in the Slides section and click OK. Then when you click the Slide Show button to deliver the presentation, only the selected slides are displayed. You can change the pen color by selecting a new color in the Pen Color edit box. (We discuss the pen in more detail on the next page.) Finally, you can click the Projector Wizard button and work through the wizard's dialog boxes to set up and fine-tune a projector to give the best on-screen slide image.

presentation itself obviously has a lot to do with its success, but a number of other factors come into play, such as the delivery style of the speaker and his or her ability to help the audience grasp the main thrust of the presentation. Also important is the speaker's ability (and willingness) to meet the audience's needs for clarification and more information. In this section, we discuss the PowerPoint features that enable you to maximize the chances that your audience will walk away from your electronic slide show having understood and accepted its message.

Drawing on the Slides

Although you have taken great pains to reduce the words on your slides to the minimum number needed to describe the point you want to get across, you may still want to draw attention to a single word (or other element) on a slide. Just as you can mark up overhead transparencies with a felt-tip marker, you can mark up electronic slides with an on-screen "pen," and you don't even have to worry about cleaning up the mess afterward.

Suppose you decide that you want to emphasize some of the airfare prices on Slide 7 of the Paranormal Tours presentation. Follow these steps to see how to mark up a slide on-the-fly:

1. In slide sorter view, choose Select All from the Edit menu. Click the Slide Transition button and deselect the Automatically After setting in the Advance section of the Slide Transition dialog box. Then click Apply To All so that you can manually move from slide to slide.

2. Click a blank area of the screen, select Slide 7, click the Slide Show button, and display both the title and the table.

3. Press Ctrl+P. (You can also right-click and choose Pointer Options and then Pen from the Slide Show shortcut menu.) The pointer is now shaped like a pen.

4. Move the pen pointer to the first item in the Airfare column, hold down the left mouse button, and draw a square or circle around $200. Then draw a square or circle around $566 at the bottom of the column. The slide now looks as shown here:

"Drill-down" files

If you have supporting information in a file created with another Windows application, you can access that information during a PowerPoint slide show by "drilling down" to it. For example, you can drill down to a report created in Word or an inventory list created in Access. The drill-down process works only with applications that support OLE (object linking and embedding). To add a drill-down file to a presentation, you embed the file as an object. First choose Object from the Insert menu. When the Insert Object dialog box appears, select the Create From File option and enter the complete path of the file in the File edit box. (If you don't know the path, click the Browse button and select the file in the Browse dialog box.) Next select the Display As Icon option and click OK. The embedded object is then displayed on the current slide as an icon. To drill down to the file, double-click the icon in slide view. The originating application starts and displays the file in a window. To return to the presentation, click the Close button on the originating application's title bar.

Typical Tour Package Prices

Paranormal Tours			
Tour	Airfare	Hotel	Transport
ET Exploration	$200	$475	$120
Ghostly B&Bs, US	$480	$695	$230
Ghostly B&Bs, Europe	$798	$1,350	$360
Bermuda Triangle	$566	$1,029	$345

Exotic Excursions   7

Try changing the color of the pen's ink:

1. Click the right mouse button and choose Pointer Options and then Pen Color from the Slide Show shortcut menu. Then select a different color from the drop-down list.

Changing the pen color

2. Draw a few more squares or circles on Slide 7.

3. Click the right mouse button and choose Pointer Options and then Arrow or press Ctrl+A to restore the arrow pointer.

Returning to the arrow pointer

PowerPoint erases the pen ink as soon as you move to the next slide in the presentation. To erase the ink before moving on to the next slide, press E. Or you can click the right mouse button and choose Screen and then Erase Pen from the shortcut menu.

Removing pen marks

Hiding Supporting Information

When someone in the audience requests clarification of a point you are making or questions your assumptions or conclusions, you will usually want to take the time to address their concerns before moving on. If you know the audience well, you can generally predict the kinds of questions they are likely to ask and can touch on those points in the presentation. But if you are unsure of the audience's level of knowledge about the topic or the focus of their interest, you probably won't want to clutter up the presentation with supporting information that the audience may not need. In that case, you might want to put the supporting information on hidden slides. Then if no questions are asked, you can simply skip over them. However, if the audience does need more information, you can display the hidden slides to qualify your statements or to provide the details.

In Chapter 2, you added a graph slide to the Paranormal Tours presentation with information about increasing public interest in paranormal phenomena. Suppose you want to hide this slide but keep it in the wings in case someone asks for data about the popularity of paranormal phenomena. Follow these steps to hide Slide 3:

1. Press Esc to return to slide sorter view and select Slide 3, the graph slide.

The Hide Slide button

2. Click the Hide Slide button on the Slide Sorter toolbar. Power-Point indicates that the slide will be hidden by putting a slash through the slide number; it doesn't hide the slide in this view.

3. Select Slide 2 and switch to slide show view.

4. Click the left mouse button to build the slide and then click again to move to the next slide. PowerPoint skips over Slide 3 and displays Slide 4.

5. Press the P key to return to Slide 2.

Displaying a hidden slide

6. Press H to display the hidden slide. (You can also click the right mouse button and choose Go and then By Title from the shortcut menu. Then from the By Title submenu, choose (3) Customer Survey to display the hidden slide, but that's a lot of steps when pressing one key does just as good a job!)

7. Press Page Up or P to move back to Slide 2 and then click the left mouse button. PowerPoint takes you to Slide 4, skipping over the hidden slide once again.

8. Press Esc to return to slide sorter view, select Slide 3, and click the Hide Slide button to toggle it off.

Branching to a Subordinate Presentation

Hidden slides are useful when you want to have information available in case you need it to make a point. However, if you want to design a presentation for multiple audiences, a better alternative is to build a core presentation and then incorporate other subordinate presentations that meet the needs of different groups. With some careful design work ahead of time, you can break down your presentations into reusable modules so that you can leverage your presentations in multiple directions.

Multipurpose presentations

As an example, suppose you want to be able to use the slides from the Sample Tours presentation in several other presentations. You can copy them from one presentation to another, but an alternate way of accomplishing the same thing without storing multiple copies of these slides in multiple presentations is to embed the Sample Tours file in each of the presentations where its slides are needed. Follow these steps to embed the Sample Tours presentation in the Paranormal Tours presentation:

1. Display Slide 5 of Paranormal Tours in slide view, click an insertion point at the end of the *Europe* subordinate item, and press Enter. Then choose Hyperlink from the Insert menu to open the Insert Hyperlink dialog box shown below:

Embedding one presentation in another

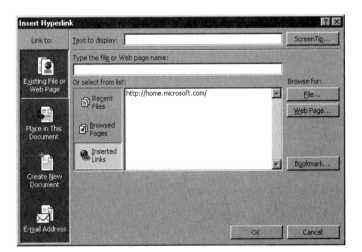

2. Click the Recent Files option and click C:\My Documents\ Sample Tours.ppt to put that file's name in the Type The File Or Web Page Name box. (If necessary, you can click File in the Browse For section and find Sample Tours.ppt that way.)

3. Change the entry in the Text To Display edit box to *Click here for details*.

4. Click OK to return to the slide, where PowerPoint has inserted a hyperlink to the Sample Tours file. Select the hyperlink text and change its size to 16 so that it will be less conspicuous. The slide now looks like this:

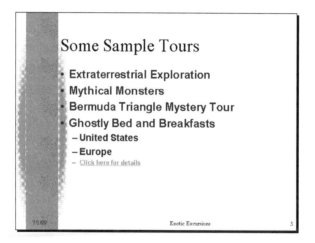

Here's another way to create a link to a different presentation:

1. Choose Picture and then From File from the Insert menu. In the Insert Picture dialog box, navigate to the folder where the graphic you originally inserted on the title slide is stored, and double-click its name. (In our case, this graphic is Ufo.bmp. If you don't have a suitable graphic, close the dialog box and draw a square or circle using one of the tools on the Drawing toolbar.)

2. Decrease the size of the graphic and drag it to the bottom right corner of the slide.

3. Now, with the graphic selected, choose Action Settings from the Slide Show menu to display the dialog box shown on the facing page.

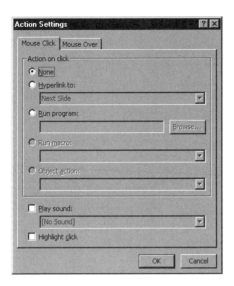

4. Click the Hyperlink To option, click the arrow to the right of the associated edit box, and select Other PowerPoint Presentation to display this dialog box:

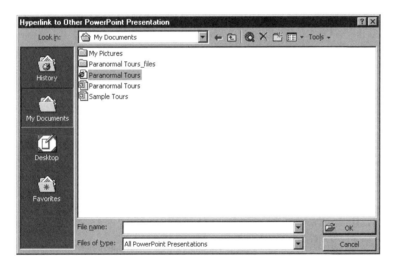

5. Double-click Sample Tours. When the Hyperlink To Slide dialog box is displayed, double-click Slide 1 and click OK.

Let's see how PowerPoint handles branching to a subordinate presentation:

1. Switch to slide show view and if necessary, click the left mouse button until all the bulleted items and the text hyperlink are displayed. Then click the text hyperlink. PowerPoint branches to the Sample Tours presentation and displays Slide 1.

Action buttons

PowerPoint's action buttons let you create hyperlinks to other slides, presentations, movies, and so on. To add a button to the current slide, choose Action Buttons from the Slide Show menu and select a button from the available palette. Then drag a frame in the area of the slide where you want the button to appear. The Action Settings dialog box automatically appears so that you can assign an action to the button.

(The slide design is very different from that of Paranormal Tours. If the presentations clash, you can change the template applied to Sample Tours at any time.)

2. Click the left mouse button to step through the remaining Sample Tours slides. Then click it again to return to Slide 5 of Paranormal Tours.

3. Now test the graphic hyperlink in the same way. As you have seen, it's easy to build linked presentations. You might want to read the tip below for ideas about how you can use this capability.

Preparing for Delivery

Some people can stand up before a group and deliver an impromptu speech that nevertheless sounds eloquent and well-reasoned. The rest of us must practice, practice, practice. Even if you are an experienced speaker, you will probably want to make sure you are prepared to handle the glitches that can arise with an electronic slide show. A tiny setback can be explained to a sympathetic audience and circumvented; an accumulation of setbacks can spell disaster.

The key to avoiding embarrassment is adequate rehearsal. With electronic slide shows, rehearsing takes two forms: one involving the pacing of your presentation, and the other involving logistics. We'll look at both forms in this section.

PowerPoint Rehearsals

The hallmarks of a planned presentation are that it starts on time, ends on time, and proceeds at an easy pace in between. It accommodates questions and relevant tangents but nevertheless sticks to the topic at hand and tells the audience what they need to know. If you have been allocated 45 minutes to give a presentation, and, using a formula of about 2 minutes per slide, you create an electronic slide show of 25 slides, you will probably be uncomfortable if you get to the last slide with 20 minutes to kill. Conversely, if you are only on Slide 20 when your time is up and you have to rush your conclusion, you will probably kick yourself for not having allowed enough time to hammer home your message.

Interactive presentations

You can create a menu of presentations for the viewer to choose from by creating hyperlinks to several presentations on a blank slide. If you use graphic hyperlinks, you can use the Text Box button on the Drawing toolbar to add descriptions. For example, you could create hyperlinks to presentations about each of several products in a general sales presentation. Viewers can then click a phrase or graphic to watch a presentation about the product that interests them.

PowerPoint can't create a powerful presentation for you, but it can help you ensure that the presentation is correctly paced. You have seen how to use the Automatically After setting in the Advance section of the Slide Transition dialog box to have PowerPoint move automatically from one slide to another. Instead of entering an arbitrary number of seconds for this setting as you did earlier, you can have PowerPoint record how long each slide stays on the screen while you rehearse the presentation, and you can then use the recorded time for each slide as its Automatically After setting. This process not only gives you an idea of how long the total presentation is (when you proceed without audience interruption) but means that you can use PowerPoint's automatic advancement through the slides to keep you on track and on time.

To record the slide timings for the Paranormal Tours presentation, follow these steps:

1. Switch to slide sorter view, select Slide 1, and click the Rehearse Timings button on the Slide Sorter toolbar. PowerPoint switches to slide show view and displays this Rehearsal toolbar in the top left corner of the slide:

The Rehearse Timings button

The clock on the right shows the accumulated time for the entire presentation and the clock on the left shows the time for the current slide.

2. Say a few pertinent sentences about the title slide of the presentation, making sure to click the left mouse button in order to display the speaker's name. Then click the mouse button or the Next button in the toolbar to move on to Slide 2. The clock on the left then resets to 0 and begins timing the second slide.

3. Repeat step 2 for the remaining slides. If you need to start over for a given slide, click the Repeat button on the Rehearsal toolbar. If you need to pause, click the Pause button. (Click it again to resume.)

4. When you reach the blank slide at the end of the presentation, press the Esc key. PowerPoint then displays the message box shown here:

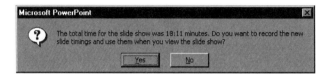

5. Make a note of the total time taken for the presentation. Then click Yes to enter the individual timings for each slide in the Slide Transition dialog box and redisplay slide sorter view, where the slides now look as shown here:

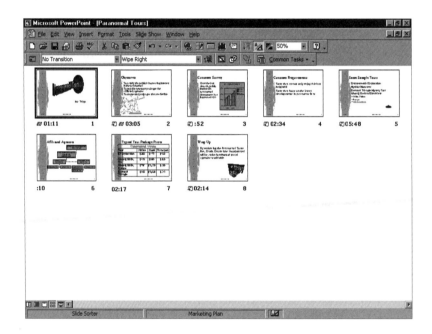

Custom slide shows

If you plan to give the same electronic slide show with slight variations to several different audiences, you can create custom slide shows to which you can branch during the presentation. Choose Custom Shows from the Slide Show menu, click the New button in the Custom Shows dialog box, and enter a name for this version of the show in the Define Custom Show dialog box. Then select the slides you want to include in this custom show and click the Add button. You can use the arrow buttons to rearrange the order of the slides. When you are done, click OK to return to the Custom Shows dialog box, where you can see a preview of the new show by clicking the Show button. To run a custom show from slide show view, simply choose Go and then Custom Show from the Slide Show shortcut menu and then select the name of the show you want.

If the total presentation time is too long, you can talk less while each slide is displayed or you can look for ways to cut the number of slides. If the time is too short, you can talk more while each slide is displayed or you can add slides. Either way, you can repeat the rehearsal process to enter new timings for each slide until you get the pace of the presentation just right. Then you need to switch from manual to automatic advancement, like this:

1. Choose Set Up Show from the Slide Show menu.

2. Check that Using Timings, If Present is selected in the Advance Slides section, and then click OK.

3. Switch to slide show view and rehearse the presentation one more time while PowerPoint runs the slide show.

If PowerPoint advances to the next slide while you are talking, you can press the S key to pause the slide show and then press either the B key to turn the screen black or the W key to turn it white while you finish what you are saying. Pressing S again resumes the show. (The Pause and Black Screen commands can also be accessed by choosing Screen from the Slide Show shortcut menu.) If you finish talking before the end of a slide's allocated display time—for example, if you allowed time for questions and there are none—you can always click the left mouse button to manually advance to the next slide. (Remember that either of these pacing adjustments will increase or decrease the total length of the presentation.)

Pausing the slide show and blanking the screen

Manually advancing an automatic slide show

Taking Care of Logistics

If you will be running your presentation under controlled conditions—in your own office using your own computer, for example, or in a familiar auditorium with equipment you have used before—you can probably skip this section. Otherwise, you should know that Murphy has a field day with electronic slide shows and that sooner or later "anything that can go wrong will go wrong." The only way to thwart Murphy's Law is to prepare adequately.

The first area to troubleshoot is the presentation equipment. Make sure you have everything you need and know how to put it together. Locate the electrical outlets in the room, set up the equipment, and check that everything is working. If someone else is in charge of setup, check in advance that they know exactly what you need, but still make a point of arriving early and, if necessary, turn on the system—just to be sure.

Next check the setup from the point of view of the audience. If you are using a projector, make sure it is the correct distance from the screen and focused to produce the sharpest image. If you are using a microphone, check its volume. Check where the light switches/dimmers are and make sure any lights that can't be dimmed do not shine directly on the screen. Also check that you can sit or stand to the side of the computer table so that you and your audience can see each other but you can also view the screen.

If you are not using your own computer, load your presentation onto the computer's hard drive ahead of time. If possible, rehearse your presentation in the room and with the equipment and lighting you will actually use.

And in case of disaster, duplicate your electronic slide show as a set of overhead transparencies and handouts and bring them with you so that you can switch to this tried-and-true format if necessary. The show must go on!

Taking a Show on the Road

Sometimes you need to deliver a presentation without knowing whether the computer that will be used has PowerPoint

Emergency accessories

Before you give an electronic slide show, remember to pack a few accessories in case of emergency:

- A checklist of all the items you need for a successful presentation (including speaker's notes and/or handouts, computer cables, mouse pointer, remote control, software and extra disks, and a sound unit/amplifier)
- Overhead transparencies or backup slides
- Small flashlight and extra batteries (so that you can find the keyboard or your notes with the lights dimmed)
- Screwdriver and small wrench (in case you have connector problems), and extra bulbs for the overhead or LCD projector (in case one burns out)
- Extension cord (so that you can reach a distant outlet)
- A backup copy of your presentation

installed on it. For these occasions, PowerPoint has a feature that ensures you have everything you need to make the electronic slide show a success. Aptly named, the Pack And Go Wizard steps you through a series of dialog boxes, asking questions about the presentation and any additional files it includes.

The Pack And Go Wizard

Let's use the Pack And Go Wizard right now to pack up the Paranormal Tours presentation so that you can run it on a computer that does not have PowerPoint:

1. Switch to slide view and save Paranormal Tours.

2. With a blank disk inserted in your floppy drive, choose Pack And Go from the File menu to display the dialog box shown below. (You may need to install the wizard first.)

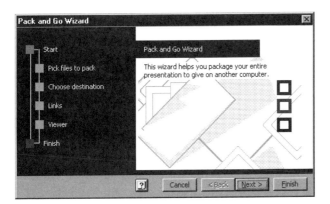

3. Click Next, check that Active Presentation is selected, and then click Next again to display the dialog box shown here:

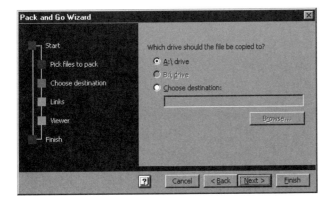

You can select a disk drive or click Choose Destination and either type the path where you want the files stored on your hard drive or simply click Browse to navigate to the destination you want.

4. Select the appropriate floppy drive letter and then click Next to display this dialog box:

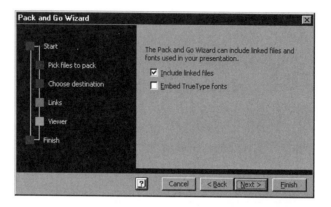

If you select Include Linked Files, any linked files will be "packed up" so that you can access them from the destination computer. If you click Embed TrueType Fonts, the wizard will embed fonts used in the presentation to ensure that text is correctly displayed if some fonts are not installed on the destination computer.

5. Leave just the Include Linked Files option selected for this exercise and then click Next to display this dialog box:

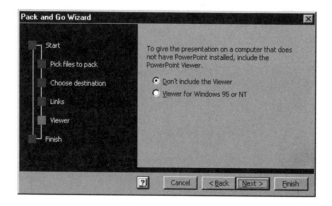

PowerPoint Viewer ⟶ If the destination computer is running Windows 95, 98, or NT but does not have PowerPoint installed, you can tell the Pack And Go Wizard to include the PowerPoint Viewer.

6. With Don't Include The Viewer selected, click Next.

7. Read the final dialog box and then click Finish. The Pack And Go Wizard packs up all the necessary files on the disk.

8. When a message box announces that the Pack And Go Wizard has finished, click OK.

9. Quit PowerPoint.

Now let's run the presentation to simulate delivering it on a destination computer. Follow these steps:

1. Create a new folder on your hard drive from which to run the presentation. (The folder's name must have eight or fewer characters and no spaces. We used the name *Present*.)

Running a presentation on another computer

2. Click the Start button on the Windows taskbar, choose Run from the Start menu, type *A:\Pngsetup*, and click OK.

3. In the Pack And Go Setup dialog box, enter the name of the destination folder you created in step 1 and click OK.

4. When a message tells you that the presentation was successfully installed, click Yes to run the show.

By now, you should feel comfortable with all the components of PowerPoint. With the skills you have learned in this book, together with the Help feature and the sample presentations that come with the program, you can tackle the creation of some pretty sophisticated presentations.

Index

Quick Course® Books

Offering beginning to intermediate training, Quick Course® books are updated regularly. For information about the most recent titles, call 1-800-854-3344 or e-mail us at quickcourse@otsiweb.com.

AVAILABLE QUICK COURSE®BOOKS		
1-58278-005-6	Quick Course® in Microsoft Access 2000	$14.95
1-879399-73-3	Quick Course® in Microsoft Access 97	$14.95
1-879399-52-0	Quick Course® in Microsoft Access 7	$14.95
1-879399-32-6	Quick Course® in Access 2	$14.95
1-58278-003-X	Quick Course® in Microsoft Excel 2000	$14.95
1-879399-71-7	Quick Course® in Microsoft Excel 97	$14.95
1-879399-51-2	Quick Course® in Microsoft Excel 7	$14.95
1-879399-28-8	Quick Course® in Excel 5	$14.95
1-58278-008-0	Quick Course® in Microsoft FrontPage 2000	$14.95
1-879399-91-1	Quick Course® in the Internet Using Microsoft Internet Explorer 5	$14.95
1-879399-68-7	Quick Course® in Microsoft Internet Explorer 4	$14.95
1-879399-67-9	Quick Course® in the Internet Using Netscape Navigator, ver. 2 & 3	$14.95
1-58278-001-3	Quick Course® in Microsoft Office 2000	$24.95
1-879399-69-5	Quick Course® in Microsoft Office 97	$24.95
1-879399-54-7	Quick Course® in Microsoft Office for Windows 95/NT	$24.95
1-879399-39-3	Quick Course® in Microsoft Office for Windows, ver. 4.3	$24.95
1-58278-006-4	Quick Course® in Microsoft Outlook 2000	$14.95
1-879399-80-6	Quick Course® in Microsoft Outlook 98	$14.95
1-58278-004-8	Quick Course® in Microsoft PowerPoint 2000	$14.95
1-879399-72-5	Quick Course® in Microsoft PowerPoint 97	$14.95
1-879399-33-4	Quick Course® in PowerPoint 4	$14.95
1-58278-007-2	Quick Course® in Microsoft Publisher 2000	$14.95
1-58278-000-5	Quick Course® in Microsoft Windows 2000	$15.95
1-879399-81-4	Quick Course® in Microsoft Windows 98	$15.95
1-879399-34-2	Quick Course® in Windows 95	$14.95
1-879399-14-8	Quick Course® in Windows 3.1	$14.95
1-879399-22-9	Quick Course® in Windows for Workgroups	$14.95
1-879399-64-4	Quick Course® in Windows NT Workstation 4	$16.95

AVAILABLE QUICK COURSE®BOOKS		
1-58278-002-1	Quick Course® in Microsoft Word 2000	$14.95
1-879399-70-9	Quick Course® in Microsoft Word 97	$14.95
1-879399-50-4	Quick Course® in Microsoft Word 7	$14.95
1-879399-27-X	Quick Course® in Word 6	$14.95
1-879399-49-0	Quick Course® in WordPerfect 6.1 for Windows	$14.95

Volume discounts available for orders of 5 or more of the same title.

Quick Course® Workbooks

Providing additional practice exercises and true/false and fill-in-the-blank quizzes, the workbooks are sold only with an accompanying Quick Course® book and in quantities of FIVE or more. Exercise and answer files are provided in an Instructor's Resource packet, which is free with orders of TEN or more workbooks.

AVAILABLE WORKBOOKS		
1-879399-78-4	Microsoft Access 97 Workbook	$11.95
1-879399-84-9	Access 97 Instructor's Resource Packet	$11.95
1-879399-77-6	Microsoft Excel 97 Workbook	$11.95
1-879399-85-7	Excel 97 Instructor's Resource Packet	$11.95
1-58278-010-2	Microsoft Office 2000 Workbook	$14.95
1-58278-014-5	Office 2000 Instructor's Resource Packet	$14.95
1-879399-74-1	Microsoft Office 97 Workbook	$14.95
1-879399-83-0	Office 97 Instructor's Resource Packet	$14.95
1-879399-65-2	Microsoft Office 95 Workbook	$14.95
1-879399-66-0	Office 95 Instructor's Resource Packet	$14.95
1-879399-46-6	Microsoft Office ver. 4.3 Workbook	$14.95
1-879399-45-8	Office 4.3 Instructor's Resource Packet	$14.95
1-879399-79-2	Microsoft PowerPoint 97 Workbook	$11.95
1-879399-86-5	PowerPoint 97 Instructor's Resource Packet	$11.95
1-879399-76-8	Microsoft Word 97 Workbook	$11.95
1-879399-87-3	Word 97 Instructor's Resource Packet	$11.95
1-879399-88-1	Microsoft Windows 98 Workbook	$12.75
1-879399-89-X	Windows 98 Instructor's Resource Packet	$12.75

Prices and availability are subject to change without notice.

Quick Course® Online Training

For those times when books alone don't quite fit the bill, Quick Course® training is now offered online.

This exciting new CD-ROM-based, interactive option incorporates video demonstrations into the acclaimed Quick Course® hands-on training format. Each title is fully searchable and includes a detailed table of contents and a comprehensive index. Document files are provided for each unit so that tasks can be tackled in the order presented in the course or on an as-needed basis. Web-based support is provided for all online courses.

Quick Course® online training can be delivered via CD-ROM, the Internet, or an intranet. It is ideal for self-paced training and can facilitate and enhance instructor-led courses. Titles are sold as individual copies or as site licenses. Please call for pricing information.

AVAILABLE IN ONLINE FORMAT
Quick Course® in Microsoft Access 2000
Quick Course® in Microsoft Excel 2000
Quick Course® in Microsoft FrontPage 2000
Quick Course® in Microsoft Office 2000
Quick Course® in Microsoft PowerPoint 2000
Quick Course® in Microsoft Publisher 2000
Quick Course® in Microsoft Word 2000